WORLD SPORTING SCANDALS

LANCASHIRE COUNTY LIBRARY	
3011812740355 2	
Askews & Holts	14-Aug-2013
796 ADA	£12.99
HBA	

First published in 2013 by
New Holland Publishers
London • Sydney • Cape Town • Auckland
www.newhollandpublishers.com

Garfield House 86–88 Edgware Road London W2 2EA United Kingdom
1/66 Gibbes Street Chatswood NSW 2067 Australia
Wembley Square First Floor Solan Road Gardens Cape Town 8001 South Africa
218 Lake Road Northcote Auckland New Zealand

Copyright © 2013 in text: Tony Adams
Copyright © 2013 in photographs: Wikimedia Commons
Copyright © 2013 New Holland Publishers

All rights reserved. No part of this publication may be reproduced, stored in a retrieval system or transmitted, in any form or by any means, electronic, mechanical, photocopying, recording or otherwise, without the prior written permission of the publishers and copyright holders.

A catalogue record of this book is available at the British Library and at the National Library of Australia.

ISBN: 9781742574011

10 9 8 7 6 5 4 3 2 1

Managing director: Fiona Schultz
Publisher: Alan Whiticker
Project editor: Kate Sherington
Designer: Kimberley Pearce
Production director: Olga Dementiev
Printer: Toppan Leefung Printing Limited

Follow New Holland Publishers on
Facebook: www.facebook.com/NewHollandPublishers

WORLD SPORTING SCANDALS

TONY ADAMS

CONTENTS

Introduction

All my life, I have been intrigued by the theatre and drama of professional sport – games all over the world produce moments of unscripted, raw emotion, sometimes sad, often touching and occasionally humorous. Sport is about much more than gold medals, records and trophies; we love the passion, the fury, the joy and the anger, too.

In professional sport, with all its tensions and pressures, scandal is never far away. Hence compiling this book, which documents some of the greatest scandals in sport over the last century and more, has been an immensely challenging and enjoyable task.

The book delves into more than 80 incidents to have rocked the sporting world, but in truth I could have covered many more. Having been a sports journalist for the past 30 years, I had already reported on several of these stories. Others I followed from afar, intrigued, as events unfolded in ever more surprising ways.

I hope you will enjoy the stories we present here. Some are amusing, others sad, and still more are simply outrageous. Many would seem to be the result of poor decisions made by athletes or officials in the heat of the moment. Others appear more cold and calculating affairs – blatant efforts at cheating, such as the Chicago White Sox's concerted game-throwing escapades in the 1919 World Series, and the tragic shooting of Columbian soccer hero Andres Escobar.

A theme among many of the scandals is the way in which sportspeople can lose their way after retirement, struggling to find their place in the world after the cheers, back-slaps and lavish contracts of their peak have become a thing of the past. It's also interesting to note that a majority of bigger scandals have occurred in recent decades, since big money came into professional sport. Vast sums of money can bring a new kind of pressure, and a 'do whatever it takes' attitude that wasn't so often seen before, when sport seemed a purer endeavour.

My thanks go to Kate Sherington and Alan Whiticker of New Holland Publishers for their enthusiastic support and guidance throughout this project. Mention must also go to Phil Rothfield of *The Daily Telegraph*, who helped develop the concept and aided me in the massive task of compiling the list of scandals to have made the cut here.

A special 'thank you' also goes to my lovely wife Toni, who was always there when I needed her between the long hours on the keyboard.

As we were finalising these books, new scandals were erupting all over the world. Plenty of material, perhaps, for a second volume.

Tony Adams
March 2013

'BLACK SOX' LIFE BAN, 1919

THE BACKGROUND

In the days immediately after the Great War, the World Series was – and still is, many believe – the grandest event in American sport. The Chicago White Sox entered the 1919 World Series as hot favourites to beat the Cincinnati Reds. But the White Sox had several players with connections to Chicago's organised mobsters, and these same players were dissatisfied

The Chicago White Sox team of 1919.

with their wages in an ongoing dispute with the controversial team owner, multi-millionaire Charles Comiskey. The club was originally dubbed 'The Black Sox' because Comiskey decided to save money by having the players' uniforms washed less often after games. Chicago did have the highest payroll in baseball in 1919, but several of the players were still on ordinary wages considering their skills. The team was also divided into two bitterly antagonistic factions – 'good-time' working class players led by first baseman Arnold Gandil, and the more educated, upper class members of the team.

Rumours had been rife for several years before 1919 that players were throwing games. Gamblers had close links to ball players, betting on baseball was common, and several former players became big gamblers and had close ties with leading stars of the day.

THE SCANDAL

Gandil allegedly conspired with close friend and professional gambler Joseph Sullivan to 'throw' several games in the series, with notorious New York gangster Arnold Rothstein bankrolling the conspiracy. Gandil then enlisted several of his team-mates from the working class players to intentionally lose to the Reds. These allegedly included key players – pitchers Eddie Cicotte and Claude Williams, and shortstop Charles Risburg. Cicotte, a star pitcher and key man in the fix, was known to be an easy target because he had financial problems, having bought a Michigan farm accompanied by a high mortgage. Several others were asked to participate, but refused.

The actual amount the players demanded from gamblers, and how much they received, has been the subject of intense debate over the years, varying from $10,000 per man to $80,000. Rumours of the fix were rife even before the series began, and as money poured in on Cincinnati, their odds plummeted. Several journalists in the press box suspected the fix was on and kept detailed notes of individual White Sox stars' efforts. Cincinnati won game one 9 to 1, and sportswriters began to smell something fishy as normally reliable Chicago players made schoolboy errors. Chicago tried a little harder in game two, but still lost 4-2. Sox catcher Roy Schalk, who was not in on the fix, bitterly complained after this game that Williams kept going against his signals.

By game three, the players were angry they hadn't received all the promised money and played their normal games, winning 3 to 0. But they threw game five, before again turning on the gamblers for failure to pay, winning games six and seven. The Reds won the series in the crucial eighth game, by 10 to 5. Williams pitched poorly, was barely used, and his wife Lyria later claimed that he was under pressure to throw the game after the gamblers threatened to harm his family.

THE AFTERMATH

Almost 12 months later, with rumours persisting, the government ordered a grand jury to investigate the sordid affair. Two players, Cicotte and the legendary 'Shoeless' Joe Jackson, confessed their involvement. Seven players were ultimately suspended by Comiskey, but key evidence, including Cicotte and Jackson's signed confessions, went missing from the courthouse and both recanted their earlier statements. The players went to trial; leading gambler 'Sleepy' Burns testified against them after being granted immunity from prosecution. They were found not guilty, but less than 24 hours later, the Commissioner of Baseball banned eight players for life, rocking American society and gutting the White Sox. It was 40 years before they won another championship.

The scandal became an integral part of American folklore, the subject of movies such as *Eight Men Out* and *Field of Dreams*. The latter focused on Jackson, who never played top-class baseball again and protested his innocence throughout his life. Many years later, several other members of the Black Sox admitted he had not been involved, although he did attend meetings as the players debated the fix. Jackson's statistics for the series back up the claim that he was wrongly convicted – he did not make a single error, batted .356 (well above his career average), got six RBIs and hit Chicago's only home run. Historians believe Jackson did take some money from the gamblers, but did not perform poorly like his team-mates. Jackson was the first of the eight to die, in 1951, aged 63.

PAKISTAN CRICKETERS JAILED, 2011

THE BACKGROUND

With close ties to bookmakers and big money gamblers, cricket on the sub-continent has been the subject of intense speculation in recent years. Players, officials and journalists have made allegations of suspicious on-field activity more than once. Some have been proven, others dismissed, but the stench of corruption lingers.

Former India captain Mohammad Azharuddin rocked the game when he was implicated in a match-fixing scandal in the 1990s and was banned for life, before being reinstated by the Indian Cricket Board several years later. Former Pakistan captain Salim Malik was banned for life by the Pakistan authorities after match-fixing allegations in 2000, but his ban was lifted in 2008. The International Cricket Council's Anti-Corruption and Security Unit has kept a close eye on Pakistan as a result and in July 2010 served two then-unnamed players with notices seeking information about spot and match-fixing. The players received the notices after England thrashed Pakistan by 354 runs in the First Test. The pair were told the ACSU was investigating specific charges and they were given two weeks in which to respond; failure to comply would itself be seen as an offence under the ICC's anti-corruption code. To add to the Pakistan team's woes, several players were also facing the prospect of investigation by their own government over tax issues.

THE SCANDAL

A month later, in August 2010, a reporter from the tabloid magazine *News of the World*, posing as a wealthy gambler, contacted a sports agent with alleged links to betting, Mazhar Majeed.

The reporter secretly filmed a conversation with Majeed in which the agent was counting money and predicting that Pakistan's Mohammad Amir would bowl the third over in the Fourth Test, played in Leeds, and would bowl a no-ball with his first ball of the over. Majeed also told the reporter that the final ball of the 10th over, bowled by Mohammad Asif, would be a no-ball.

Both deliveries, as it turned out, were no-balls as predicted, where the bowler's foot lands in front of the line that marks the crease.

The Pakistan Cricket Board was quick to defend the three players named by *The News of the World* – Asif, Amir and Salman Butt – insisting they were innocent. The players also denied any knowledge of a sting, but were suspended by the International Cricket Council pending an investigation in September. The ICC ruled the players had "an arguable case to answer", a decision that prompted the Pakistani High Commissioner to the UK to claim they had been "set up". All three players filed appeals to have their suspensions lifted, with the ICC holding a hearing in the United Arab Emirates in late October. Asif withdrew his appeal, saying he wanted to fully understand the charges against him, while Butt and Amir had their initial appeals rejected. In February 2011, an ICC tribunal subsequently banned Butt for 10 years (five suspended), Asif for seven years (two suspended) and Amir for five years.

THE AFTERMATH

Scotland Yard stepped in, arresting Majeed on charges of allegedly defrauding bookmakers. Three more people were arrested in relation to the case, on money laundering charges. Police seized the mobile phones of the three players as the Crown mounted a case against them. In November 2011, Southwark Crown Court found the three players and Majeed guilty of conspiracy to cheat at gambling and conspiracy to accept corrupt payments.

The verdicts shocked Pakistan. Former national captain Aamer Sohail declared it was a shameful day for Pakistani cricket, declaring, "This is what happens when you don't react quickly enough to fight corruption." Two days after being found guilty, the sentences were announced – Butt received 30 months in jail, Asif got one year, Amir six months and Majeed the heaviest sentence of two years and eight months. "It is the insidious effect of your actions on professional cricket and the followers of it that makes the offences so serious," Justice Cooke said.

British tax officials also opened an investigation into Croydon Athletic Football Club, which Majeed bought in 2008 and was allegedly using as a money-laundering facility. The club manager and his assistant subsequently left the club, while the chairman, David Le Cluse, was shot dead in October 2010. After a police investigation, his death was determined to be suicide.

Allegations of spot and match-fixing continue to haunt Pakistani cricket, with several players under suspicion. In November 2010, wicketkeeper Zulqarnain Haider fled the team camp in Dubai, flying to London and asking for asylum. He retired from cricket, claiming he received death threats after refusing to fix games. Haider subsequently withdrew the allegations, was fined by Pakistan officials and resumed playing.

FINE COTTON'S PAINTED SUBSTITUTE, 1984

THE BACKGROUND

Fine Cotton was a little-known Australian racehorse with a very modest record in Queensland racing in the early 1980s. Because of his poor performances, he was eligible to compete in restricted races – those for horses without many wins – and still struggled. In what was ostensibly his last run, Fine Cotton finished 10th out of 12 horses over 1200 metres at Brisbane's Doomben track in August, 1984. He started at 20-1, attracted little interest, and would barely have troubled bookies had he been 100-1.

A syndicate of punters decided to buy a horse that looked identical to Fine Cotton to the untrained eye, but had a far more impressive track record. They planned to substitute the horse, Dashing Solitaire, for Fine Cotton at another Brisbane track, Eagle Farm, 10 days after his previous race, and bet heavily on the improved horse at long odds. But the plan fell apart when Dashing Solitaire got injured in a training accident and was unable to race. Instead of scrapping the plan, the syndicate decided to go ahead regardless and went in search of another 'ring-in'. They quickly found another horse, Bold Personality, but had an immediate problem – the horse had no markings while Fine Cotton had white markings on his hind legs. They applied hair colouring to Bold Personality's legs, followed by white paint.

THE SCANDAL

The race chosen for 'Fine Cotton' was a novice handicap for horses with few wins, one that Bold Personality was not eligible for, in 1984. The bookies had Fine Cotton at 33-1 in initial markets but money started to pour in from all around the country, as word of 'the sting' began to spread. By the time the race began, the horse's odds were slashed to 7-2, making him equal favourite. The syndicate behind the ruse stood to make over $1.5 million if the horse won, but the huge amounts being thrown on a horse with no form sent alarm bells ringing in the heads of racing officials. Even in Sydney, the large amounts wagered on the unfancied gelding had bookmakers talking. Fine Cotton/Bold Personality began the race slowly, but jockey Gus Philpot soon made up lost ground. It became a two-horse race with Harbour Gold, the early favourite. In the end, Fine Cotton/Bold Personality won, but only by a nose thanks to a desperate lunge at the finish.

But before punters could collect their cash, stewards sprung into action. They noticed the paint beginning to run on the horse's leg. Several spectators in the vicinity began chanting "ring-in". They interviewed trainer Hayden Haitana and asked for the horse's papers to confirm the true identity of the winner. Haitiana couldn't produce them and Fine Cotton was promptly disqualified, with Harbour Gold awarded the race. Those who backed Fine Cotton never received a cent.

THE AFTERMATH

Police went after Haitana and he was eventually tracked down in South Australia. He and the alleged mastermind of the scheme, John 'The Phantom' Gillespie, were tried and sentenced to jail terms. Eight other people, including prominent bookmakers Bill and Robbie Waterhouse, were 'warned off' (the racing term for banned) for life. The Waterhouses' ban was lifted in 1998 after 14 years.

Haitana served six months of a 12-month sentence but his life ban has remained intact, despite several appeals by the disgraced trainer. Haitana still can't even attend a racetrack, let alone get his trainer's license back. "I'm a senior so I should get my concession. But if I show them my ID to prove it, then they won't let me in," Haitana said in an interview in 2010. Haitana insists the real truth, and other big names involved, has yet to come out, and that he was just a pawn in the scheme. "I didn't nominate the horse, I didn't book the jockey," he declared. "I tried to hide but I was stuffed." Ironically, Haitana's last 'legal' win came while he was operating under a stay of proceedings in 1984 in Sydney, on a rank $201 outsider, Roimac. He now does odd jobs in South Australia.

Fine Cotton was bought by movie producer John Stainton just a year after the scandal in 1985. "I bought the rights to the story and bought Fine Cotton to star as himself in the movie," Stainton explained. "But it was a legal minefield and I had to shelve the movie." Fine Cotton died in 2009, aged 31, and remains one of Australia's most famous horses despite his modest record.

BODYLINE, 1932

THE BACKGROUND

When the English cricket team arrived in Australia in the summer of 1932–33, they knew one man stood between them and the Ashes – local superstar Don Bradman. Three years earlier, Bradman had almost single-handedly won Australia the Ashes trophy, scoring 974 runs in the series at an average of an astounding 139, a record that has never been broken. Bradman was

The English 'Bodyline' team.

the best batsman the world had seen and the English were desperate to come up with a way to curb his brilliance. And it was in their search that the controversial tactic of 'Bodyline', in which the bowlers deliberately aimed the ball at the batsman's head and chest, and set field accordingly, was born. The theory was that such bowling prevented batsmen from playing attacking shots, and in self-preservation they would spoon easy catches to the cordon of fielders on the onside. Bradman had appeared vulnerable to short-pitched bowling in the past and England captain Douglas Jardine was determined to exploit this perceived weakness to its fullest.

THE SCANDAL

The Englishmen, who preferred to call Bodyline 'fast leg theory bowling', began using the controversial tactic early in the tour with some success. With Bradman absent through illness, the English romped to a 10-wicket win in the First Test in Sydney, with the Australian batsmen unable to cope with this new, intimidating form of bowling. Fearsome bowler Harold Larwood, the spearhead of the tourists' attack, led the way with 10 wickets. Bradman was passed fit for the Second Test in Melbourne, and was famously bowled first ball when he wildly hooked at a loose delivery. Bradman recovered his composure to score a century in the second innings as the home side levelled the series at one-all. But it was to be Bradman's only century of the series and his scores were well down on his usual huge numbers.

Bodyline reached its ugly climax in the Third Test in Adelaide when Australian captain Bill Woodfull suffered a series of painful blows to the body from short-pitched deliveries. The crowd booed and heckled the English bowlers as they continued to aim missiles at his bruised ribs, and there were fears of a riot as feelings ran high. When English manager Pelham Warner later visited the Australian dressing room to check on Woodfull's condition, the Aussie captain famously declared, "There are two teams out there ... but only one is playing cricket." The following day, Aussie batsman Bert Oldfield had his skull fractured by a thunderous delivery from Larwood. Australian officials sent a strongly worded telegram to their English counterparts in London, stating antagonism caused by Bodyline was running so high that it "is likely to upset friendly relations existing between our two countries".

The Englishmen went on to win the series by four Tests to one, with the English officials and public, who could not see the unsavoury tactics first-hand, convinced the Australians were merely sore losers.

Several of the English players, notably fast bowler Gubby Allen, were opposed to Bodyline. Allen refused to bowl at the batsman's body despite being ordered to do so by Jardine, and was highly critical of the tactic in later years.

THE AFTERMATH

The laws of cricket were changed in 1935, two years after the tour, to stamp out Bodyline bowling forever, but tensions between the two nations (and their representative cricket players) continued to run high. English officials asked Larwood to sign an apology to them for the way he bowled on the tour. He refused, declaring he was merely following the orders of Jardine, and never played for England again. Ironically, Larwood, the man regarded as the face of Bodyline, moved to Australia in the 1950s, where he died in 1995 at the age of 91. Jardine defended the tactics throughout his life, claiming allegations he set out to hurt rival batsmen were absurd. Ill feeling continued in Australia for several years after the Bodyline series, with English immigrants given a hostile reception by the locals. Commerce between the two nations, traditionally the closest of allies, also suffered. International relations remained strained until the outbreak of World War II in 1939, when both countries realised there were more important battles to be fought.

Bodyline is considered such a significant event in Australian history that it has at times been included in the modern history syllabus in schools.

NFL STAR'S DEAD GIRLFRIEND HOAX, 2013

THE BACKGROUND

Manti Te'o is rated among the most talented footballers the state of Hawaii has ever produced. Born in 1991, he grew up on Oahu and was a star high school linebacker at the Punahou School. He was named State Defensive Player of the Year and Gatorade State Player of the Year in 2007. As well as playing on the defence, he scored 10 touchdowns as a running back. In his senior year in 2008, he had colleges falling over themselves to recruit him, as he led Punahou to its first state championship. He won the inaugural Butkus Award as the best linebacker in the country and *Sporting News* named him the High School Athlete of the Year.

Te'o joined the University of Notre Dame for 2009, immediately shining in his freshman season. He led the Fighting Irish in tackles in both 2010 and 2011 and won numerous awards for his aggressive style. In 2012, his senior year, he led Notre Dame to the BCS championship game and became the most decorated defensive player in college football history, finishing second in Heisman Trophy voting.

Te'o became even more beloved and admired in September 2012, when he revealed his grandmother and girlfriend had both died in the space of 24 hours. He made front page news after tearfully telling of how his girlfriend Lennay Kekua had died after suffering from leukemia. He played on through the tragedy, refusing to miss any games, saying it was what Lennay wanted.

THE SCANDAL

Sporting blog *Deadspin* received an anonymous tip early in 2013 that something in Te'o's story did not add up. On 16 January, two reporters were put on the story and published a report that they could find no record of any woman called Lennay Kekua, dead or alive. They found that the photos published nationwide of Kekua were in fact those of another woman, Diane O'Meara, an acquaintance of one of Te'o's friends, Ronaiah Tuiasosopo.

Notre Dame immediately went into damage control, stating that Te'o had been "the victim of what appears to be a hoax in which someone using the fictitious name Lennay Kekua apparently ingratiated herself with Manti and then conspired with others to lead him to believe she had tragically died of leukemia." The university's athletic director, Jack Swarbrick, told the media he had hired a private detective to look into the matter, and that he had reported that the relationship between Te'o and Kekua was purely online – they had never met. This contradicted Te'o's father Brian's own account of the relationship; he had earlier stated the pair met after a game and that Kekua had visited his son in Hawaii.

Swarbrick added that Te'o informed the school of the hoax on 26 December after receiving a call 20 days earlier from the woman he thought to be Kekua, weeks after her supposed death, claiming she was still alive. Despite this, he continued to perpetuate the myth of his 'dead girlfriend' in several media interviews after that phone call.

THE AFTERMATH

The story went global, with Te'o suspected of being involved in the hoax. In an attempt to clear his name, he gave an interview to renowned sports reporter Jeremy Schaap, insisting he was an innocent victim in a cruel con job. He explained that he had lied to people, including his family, about meeting Kekua because he believed they would have labelled him crazy for having such a serious relationship with a woman he had only met online. He alleged he was left stunned by the 6 December phone call, and that he continued to refer to Kekua as his 'dead girlfriend' because he was hurt and confused. He said he had met Tuiasosopo, who introduced himself as Kekua's cousin, and alleged that Tuiasosopo had eventually admitted he was the one behind the entire hoax.

Tuiasosopo, the alleged mastermind of the ruse, later said he did not plan to hurt Te'o. "He did not intend to harm him in any way," his attorney, Milton Grimes, said. Tuiasosopo was planning to come clean in a television interview, Lance Armstrong-style. Tuiasosopo even admitted to faking Kekua's voice in alleged phone conversations with Te'o. "I don't think it's so unusual that a person could imitate the voice of a person of a different sex," Grimes said. Grimes added that his client "feels as though he needs therapy and part of that therapy is to ... tell the truth."

On 31 January, Tuiasosopo spoke to Dr Phil. He claimed that Te'o had no idea he was being conned, and also admitted to having feelings for the footballer, saying, "As twisted and confusing as it may be, yeah, I cared for this person [Te'o]. I did all that I could to help this person become a better person, even though I wasn't getting nothing out of it."

NBA REF'S BETTING SHAME, 2007

THE BACKGROUND

Tim Donaghy was among the American National Basketball Association's leading referees in the 1990s and 2000s. Born in Pennsylvania in 1967, Donaghy started his career in high school games in his home state in the 1980s before becoming a leading official with the Continental Basketball Association. He graduated to the NBA in 1994, quickly establishing himself as a regular and officiating in over 750 regular-season games and 20 playoff matches.

He was involved in a controversial incident in 2003 when he called a technical foul on Portland Trail Blazers star Rasheed Wallace for allegedly throwing a ball at another referee. The pair had an ugly confrontation after the game, in which Wallace allegedly yelled obscenities at the referee. Wallace was suspended for seven games, at the time the longest suspension in NBA history for an incident not involving drugs or violence. He also handled an infamous Pacers v Pistons clash in 2004 that saw fighting between Pacers players and Pistons fans.

THE SCANDAL

In July 2007, the *New York Post* broke a story about the FBI investigating allegations that an NBA referee had bet on games in respect to the points spread. The paper alleged Donaghy had a gambling problem and had bet six-figure sums on games in the 2005–06 and 2006–07 seasons. It said the FBI was actually conducting a wider investigation into mob involvement in sports betting when it stumbled on Donaghy's involvement.

Donaghy resigned from the game, leaving the NBA stunned by the allegations and launching its own internal investigation. "This is a wake-up call that says you can't be complacent," a worried NBA commissioner David Stern said. Sports betting experts began analysing games which Donaghy had officiated, finding teams scored more points that expected by bookies 57 percent of the time, compared to 44 percent in the previous two seasons. They also found big money going on 10 straight Donaghy games in 2007, with the punters winning on almost every occasion.

In August, Donaghy pleaded guilty to conspiracy to engage in wire fraud and transmitting betting information via interstate commerce. He told the US District Court that he used code to relay information to a bookie about player fitness and player/referee relations. He allegedly received amounts varying from $2,000 to $30,000 for this information. It was also revealed Donaghy had a gambling addiction and was taking antidepressant medication. He admitted to passing on the information and prosecutors also alleged he had bet on games himself. In June 2008, Donaghy returned fire with a bombshell of his own, filing a court document alleging the NBA used referees to manipulate finals games to extend series to seven games. NBA Commissioner Stern strongly denied the allegations.

THE AFTERMATH

Donaghy was fined $500,000 and was also ordered to pay restitution. He was released on $250,000 bond and in July 2008 was sentenced to 15 months in prison. Judge Carol Amon could have imposed a 33-month sentence, but more than halved it because of Donaghy's cooperation. "The NBA, the players and the fans relied on him to perform his job in an honest manner," Judge Amon said. In court, Donaghy admitted his error: "I brought shame on myself, my family and my profession."

The scandal made the NBA take a deep look at its officials, with Stern changing the guidelines on referee behaviour. Gambling rules for referees were relaxed to allow referees to engage in several forms of casino betting, but not sports betting. Counselling of referees and background checks were also stepped up. The scandal shook the NBA to its core, with players stunned by the affair. "As a competitor, as hard as I play, it is disappointing, definitely," superstar LeBron James said.

Donaghy wrote his memoirs while serving time in a federal prison in Pensacola, Florida. After 11 months, he was released to a recovery house, but was arrested after attending a health club without permission and returned to jail to finish his sentence.

Donaghy insists he never fixed games. "I didn't need to fix them," he argued in his book. "I usually knew which team was going to win based on which referees had been assigned to the game, their personalities and the relationships they had with the players and coaches of the teams involved."

FBI investigations appeared to back up Donaghy's claims, finding that his actual officiating was not compromised, despite the fact he wagered on games.

O.J. ESCAPES MURDER CONVICTION, 1995

THE BACKGROUND

Orenthal James 'O. J.' Simpson was a brilliant college and professional footballer. An athletic running back, Simpson holds a special place in the game's history as the first NFL player to rush for more than 2,000 yards in a season. While several players have gone on to emulate Simpson's 1973 landmark, none have done it in a 14-game season, with the NFL switching to 16 games in 1978.

Simpson, depicted here in 1990.

Born in San Francisco in 1947, Simpson suffered from rickets and wore braces on his legs until the age of five. He overcame this to shine in football and on the track as a teenager, winning an athletic scholarship at the University of Southern California, where he led the nation in rushing in 1967 and 1968, winning the Heisman Trophy in the latter year. He also ran as a sprinter and was part of the 4 x 110 yard relay team that broke the world record in the 1967 NCAA championships. He was drafted by Buffalo in 1969 and after struggling early in a poor Bills team, shone in the early to mid-1970s.

Known throughout the US as 'Juice', Simpson played his final two seasons with San Francisco in 1978–79 before retiring, earning induction into the Pro Football Hall of Fame in 1985. After football, Simpson became an actor, starring in movies including *The Naked Gun* series, *Capricorn One* and the mini-series *Roots*. Handsome and articulate, he also became a popular commentator on football for the NBC network.

THE SCANDAL

On the night of 12 June 1994, Simpson's former wife Nicole Brown and her friend Ron Goldman were murdered outside her Los Angeles house. Simpson became a suspect and his lawyers agreed with the Los Angeles Police Department that he would turn himself in, five days after the murders. Simpson failed to show at the 2pm deadline, with one of his defence lawyers reading a statement from the former star, in which he denied any involvement in the crime.

Four hours later, police spotted Simpson and a friend driving around the streets of Orange County in a while Ford Bronco. The driver, Simpson's friend A. C. Cowling, told police Simpson was in the back seat with a gun to his head. Over 20 helicopters, countless police cars and thousands of people on the streets then witnessed a bizarre chase before Simpson finally surrendered, two hours later.

Simpson was charged to stand trial for Brown and Goldman's murders. One witness allegedly told police she saw his car speeding from the scene, while another claimed that he had sold Simpson a knife similar to the one used to stab Brown, but neither were called by the prosecution after having sold their stories to the media. The trial lasted 134 days and became a media circus.

In October 1995, the jury deliberated for four hours before returning a verdict of not guilty. Over 100 million people worldwide are believed to have watched or listened to the verdict.

THE AFTERMATH

In 1997, a civil court in California found Simpson liable for battery against his ex-wife and for wrongful death and battery against Goldman. He was ordered to pay over $33 million in damages, although it is believed little of the money has actually been paid.

In 2007, Simpson and several friends entered a Las Vegas hotel room, taking several pieces of valuable sports memorabilia at gunpoint. Simpson denied the robbery had been at gunpoint. He was released, then arrested two days later, charged with criminal conspiracy, kidnapping, assault and robbery, as well as using a deadly weapon. All three of his co-defendants accepted plea bargains with prosecutors in exchange for their testimony against Simpson, in which they said there were in fact guns used in the robbery.

Simpson was tried on 12 charges, pleading not guilty. He was found guilty on all charges in late 2008, and sentenced to a total of 33 years in jail, with no possibility of parole for at least nine years. He lost an appeal and is currently serving his sentence in a Nevada correctional facility. But late in 2012, a Nevada judge gave Simpson a glimmer of hope, reopening the case to determine if the former superstar had been properly represented by his legal team.

THE NAZI OLYMPICS, 1936

THE BACKGROUND

In 1931, two years before the Nazis came to power in Germany, the International Olympic Committee met in Barcelona and awarded the 1936 Olympic Games to Berlin. The Germans built a huge 100,000-seat athletic stadium as the centrepiece of their Games, as well as a host of impressive indoor venues. The Games were also the first to be shown on television, taking

Germany enters the arena at the 1936 Olympics in Berlin.

the Olympics to the widest audience in history to that point.

But as the Nazis took over the country, Hitler saw the Olympics as the ideal opportunity to spread his views of Aryan racial supremacy to the watching world. His official Nazi newsletter didn't try to disguise his twisted views, declaring that Jews and black people should be barred from competing.

With the Nazis' treatment of ethnic minorities becoming more apparent, several countries considered not taking part in the Games. American president Theodore Roosevelt and US Olympic Committee chief Avery Brundage declared their country would participate, despite some resistance, with several star American athletes choosing to boycott the Games. In the end, of the traditional Olympic participants only Spain and the Soviet Union stayed away, with the 1936 Games attracting the most countries ever up to that time.

THE SCANDAL

There were countless examples of controversy during the Games, starting on the opening day. When an American won the first gold medal on the track, Hitler, who had met several of the earlier winners, abruptly left the stadium. Olympic officials admonished the German chancellor and dictator, telling him he would have to acknowledge all winners or none at all. From that point, Hitler chose the latter. The following day, black American superstar Jesse Owens won the first of his four gold medals. Thus, contrary to legend, Hitler did not actually snub Owens – his mind had already been made up.

American sprinters Sam Stoller and Marty Glickman, both Jewish, starred in the early rounds of the 4 x 100m relay on the track but were withdrawn from the final only hours before the race. No explanation was given and many believe Brundage did this to avoid further embarrassing Hitler by allowing two Jewish runners to win gold medals.

In the cycling sprint final, German Toni Merkens appeared to foul his Dutch opponent. An inquiry found Merkens at fault, but he was allowed to keep his gold medal and merely paid a fine. In the marathon, Koreans Son Kitei and Nan Shoryu won gold and silver respectively, but competed for Japan, which had invaded and occupied Korea years earlier.

Most shocking of all, before the Olympics even began, the Nazis had rounded up gypsies and other 'undesirables', locking them out of sight in concentration camps.

THE AFTERMATH

Debate remains over whether major countries, particularly the United States, should have supported and participated in the 1936 Olympics, which was in effect a highly successful Nazi propaganda exercise. The American ambassadors to both Germany and Austria recommended the country pull out of the Games, as did several politicians on the home front, but they were ignored.

Owens, who often found himself a second-class citizen in his own country, had more of a problem with US President Franklin Roosevelt. "Hitler didn't snub me. It was FDR who snubbed me," Owens said years later. "The President didn't even send me a telegram." While Owens received a ticker-tape parade in both New York and Cleveland, he was never invited to the White House or acknowledged by Roosevelt. It wasn't until 1955, 19 years later, that he received presidential recognition from Dwight Eisenhower, who named him a Sports Ambassador.

Years later, the Nazi Minister of Armaments and War Production, Albert Speer gave a clear indication of Hitler's mindset during the Games. "He was highly annoyed by the series of triumphs by the marvellous coloured American runner Owens," Speer wrote. "'People whose antecedents came from the jungle were primitive,' Hitler said with a shrug. 'Their physiques were stronger than those of civilised whites and hence should be excluded from future games.'"

Three years after the Olympics, Germany invaded Poland, starting World War II – a six-year conflict that cost millions of lives.

DEATH AT SEA, 1998

THE BACKGROUND

The Sydney to Hobart Yacht Race is one of Australia's great sporting traditions. First held in 1945, it is a gruelling 630-nautical-mile trek run by the Cruising Yacht Club of Australia. The race begins at noon on 26 December, with a flotilla of yachts leaving Sydney Harbour, waved off by a massive crowd of other boats and well-wishers along the shore. The fleet heads down the New South Wales coast, through the Tasman Sea, past Bass Strait and up Tasmania's Derwent River before crossing the finish line in Hobart. The course is one of the most challenging in the world and tests even the best and most experienced mariners.

In 1998, 115 yachts signed up for the event. After the fleet left Sydney Harbour and were at the mercy of the open seas, a massive low-pressure depression developed (it caused snow in parts of south-eastern Australia, an extremely rare occurrence at the height of the Aussie summer). Another effect of the depression was that it whipped up powerful winds, measuring up to 70 knots in some places.

THE SCANDAL

When the storm hit the hapless boats in open water, it had reached hurricane strength. The winds created a huge and deadly waterspout, resulting in massive seas and the subsequent sinking of five boats. As the full extent of the storm became known, rescue boats raced to save the remains of the struggling fleet. But it was too late for some, with six sailors dead in the treacherous seas – Phillip Skeggs and Bruce Guy (both on board *Business Post Naiad*), John Dean, Jim Lawler and Michael Bannister (on the *Winston Churchill*) and Glyn Charles (*Sword of*

Orion). And it could have been much worse; heroic rescuers plucked 55 more sailors from the bubbling water, most by helicopter. Some 35 military and civilian aircraft were involved in the rescue, along with 27 Royal Australian Navy boats in what was, at the time, Australia's largest peacetime rescue mission.

THE AFTERMATH

Just 44 boats limped into Hobart, with US maxi yacht *Sayonara*, owned by Larry Ellison, the first across the finish line. *Midnight Rambler*, owned by Ed Psaltis and Bob Thomas, came in tenth but was declared the overall winner on handicap, as the smallest boat to win the classic in over a decade.

The New South Wales coroner John Abernethy held an official inquest into the disaster. Two weeks before the start of the 2000 Sydney to Hobart race, he handed down his findings. He was scathing of both race officials and the Bureau of Meteorology that issued the pre-race weather forecasts, declaring that the Cruising Yacht Club of Australia had "abdicated its responsibility to manage the race". In a detailed and long-reaching report, he added, "From what I have read and heard, it is clear to me that during this crucial time the race management team played the role of observers rather than managers and that was simply not good enough." He did, however, praise the CYC for the safety precautions it took in the wake of the tragedy, which included tightening crew eligibility rules, introducing minimum age and experience guidelines, and greater safety measures. He said the Bureau of Meteorology should have done more to warn the CYC, an upgraded forecast on the huge storm on the New South Wales–Victoria border having been received some 24 hours before the fleet was due there. He stipulated that the Bureau should include maximum wind gusts and wave heights in its bulletins.

Race director Phil Thompson resigned the day after the report was released. "Mr Thompson's inability to appreciate the problems when they arose and his inability to appreciate them at the time of giving his evidence causes me concern that [he] may not appreciate such problems as they arise in the future," Abernethy said.

In 2005, several relatives of the sailors who lost their lives took legal action against the CYC. After an emotional seven-day hearing, the two parties settled the case, the terms of which remain confidential. "Always my primary aim was to be vindicated, and to acknowledge the importance of my husband's life," said Denise Lawler, whose husband Jim was among the six victims of the tragedy. "That they didn't settle before only strengthened our resolve to pursue it as far as we could. Furthermore, any amendments to racing yachting rules to make it safer for everybody, as a result of this, gives our husbands' deaths some meaning."

ACCUSATION OF ON-PITCH INSULT, 2011

THE BACKGROUND

John Terry is one of the most accomplished soccer players of the modern era, and also one of the most controversial. Born in London in 1980, he came through West Ham's junior system before transferring to Chelsea, for whom he made his debut as a teenager in 1998. After a brief loan stint with Nottingham Forest in 2000, Terry established himself as a regular at the heart of the Chelsea defence. By 2004–05, he was Chelsea captain, and led the Blues to the premier league title in a record-breaking season for the club.

Terry, pictured on the field after a premiership win.

Terry has gone on to play over 500 games for Chelsea, establishing himself as the club's most successful captain, with three premier league titles, four FA Cups, two League Cups and a UEFA Champions League trophy. He won the title of UEFA Club Defender of the Year three times in the 2000s. Terry was appointed captain of England in 2006 and held the post until 2010.

Early in 2010, allegations surfaced in the press that Terry had been involved in an affair with French underwear model Vanessa Perroncel, the former girlfriend of his ex-team-mate Wayne Bridges. Perroncel vehemently denied the allegations and two British tabloid newspapers printed apologies to her. The scandal became so heated that Fabio Capello, then England manager, took the captaincy from Terry. The Chelsea star won the captaincy back 13 months later.

THE SCANDAL

English police launched an investigation following a match between Chelsea and Queens Park Rangers late in 2011. QPR star Anton Ferdinand alleged that Terry had racially abused him during a fiery clash on the pitch. Allegedly, video footage appeared to show Terry using the words "f*cking black c*nt".

Terry denied the accusations, putting out a statement saying, "I thought Anton was accusing me of using a racist slur against him. I responded aggressively, saying that I never used that term."

The following day, police received an anonymous complaint from a member of the public over the incident, with QPR also lodging an official complaint with the Football Association. The FA interviewed Ferdinand, who pushed for a full investigation. Police then got involved, passing the matter on to the Crown Prosecutor's Service, who announced in December that Terry would be charged with racially abusing Ferdinand. In February 2012, Terry's lawyers entered a plea of not guilty on his behalf at Westminster Magistrates' Court. Two days later, the FA stripped Terry of the England captaincy a second time, declaring he would not lead the team until the case was resolved. The same week, England manager Capello resigned, slamming the decision to strip Terry of the captaincy.

The case went to court in July 2012, with Terry being cleared of the charges.

THE AFTERMATH

The matter didn't end there, however. Two weeks later, the FA charged Terry with having used abusive and/or insulting behaviour towards Ferdinand. Terry was given a personal hearing to put his side of the story and firmly denied the charge. The Chelsea defender was recalled to the England squad in August for the upcoming World Cup qualifying games. The day before he was due to face the FA to defend the charge, Terry announced his retirement from international football, saying his position had become "untenable" in the wake of the dispute with the FA.

Terry was banned for four matches and fined £220,000 by the FA. The Independent Regulatory Commission appointed by the FA labelled Terry's defence as "improbable, implausible and contrived", but also concluded that Terry was not a racist. They rejected Terry's claims that he uttered the words as a forceful denial.

Terry decided not to appeal against the verdict and issued an apology for the language he used on the field. In a statement, Terry said it was "not acceptable on the football field or indeed in any walk of life".

In September 2012, when QPR next met Chelsea, Ferdinand refused to shake Terry's hand at the customary pre-match greeting, as well as that of Ashley Cole, who appeared as a character witness for Terry.

Some believed Terry had been harshly dealt with, labelling the FA's tribunal a kangaroo court, which convicted Terry after he had been cleared in a criminal court. Others believed the penalty was a just one.

TIGER'S FALL FROM GRACE, 2009

THE BACKGROUND

Tiger Woods at a press conference, earlier in 2009.

Tiger Woods is the most famous golfer – perhaps the most famous sportsman – of the new millennium. Born in California in 1975, he was a child prodigy who started swinging clubs under the watchful eye of his father Earl at the age of just two. He won the world junior championship six times before turning professional in 1996. Sponsors flocked to Woods, including heavy hitters Nike and Titleist, and the youngster lived up to the hype, winning the PGA Tour Rookie of the Year award and *Sports Illustrated*'s Sportsman of the Year in that first year. He won his first major in 1997, becoming the youngest holder of the US Masters, and in 2000 won six consecutive tournaments, the longest winning streak on the PGA Tour since 1948. By 2008, he had 14 majors to his name and 74 PGA Tour wins, and had spent more time than any other golfer at number one in the world. In 2003, he married Erin Nordegren in Barbados and the pair settled into a home in Orlando, Florida. The marriage produced two children, daughter Sam, born in 2007, and son Charlie, born in 2009. Woods appeared to be the perfect family man.

THE SCANDAL

Late in November 2009, tabloid newspaper *The National Enquirer* published a story alleging Woods had engaged in an extra-marital affair with Rachel Uchitel, a nightclub manager from New York City. Ms Uchitel denied the story. Two days later, in the early hours of the morning, Woods was involved in a car accident when his Cadillac SUV collided with a tree and a fire hydrant near his home. Woods received minor facial cuts and there was intense media speculation as to the cause. Woods was charged with careless driving and fined $164. He placed a statement on his website taking full responsibility for the crash, calling it a "private matter" and begging to be left alone by the prying media.

In early December, *US Weekly* magazine printed a story from a Californian cocktail waitress, Jaimee Grubb. She had allegedly been involved in a long-running affair with Woods and claimed to have a series of text messages that proved it. A phone message was also released, in which a man, alleged to be Woods, said to Grubb: "Um, can you please, uh, take your name off your phone. My wife went through my phone and, uh, may be calling you." Several other women also claimed to have had sexual encounters with the golfing superstar.

Woods put out a statement on his website, declaring, "I have not been true to my values and the behavior my family deserves. I have let my family down and I regret those transgressions with all of my heart."

Woods released another statement on 11 December, admitting infidelity for the first time. "I am deeply aware of the disappointment and hurt that my infidelity has caused to so many people, most of all my wife and children," he said. Woods also announced he would not play in any more tournaments in the final weeks of 2009, apparently due to the extent of his injuries from the car crash.

THE AFTERMATH

In February 2010, Woods went on television, declaring he had completed a 45-day program of therapy. He again apologised for his actions, stating, "I thought I could get away with whatever I wanted to ... I felt that I had worked hard my entire life and deserved to enjoy all the temptations around me. I felt I was entitled. Thanks to money and fame, I didn't have to go far to find them. I was wrong. I was foolish."

Several of Woods' sponsors dumped him after the shock revelations, although two of his most lucrative deals, with Nike and Electronic Arts, remained intact. Many fellow players publicly supported Woods, but Swedish star Jesper Parnevik, who introduced Woods to Nordegren years earlier, declared, "I told her this is the guy that I think is everything you want. He's true. He's honest. He has great values. He has everything you would want in a guy ... And, uhh, I was wrong," Parnevik said.

Woods and Nordegren divorced in August, 2010. Woods had returned to competitive golf four months earlier, but has not since managed to regain his status as the game's number one player.

TRAGEDY AT HILLSBOROUGH, 1989

THE BACKGROUND

The rise of hooliganism and pitch invasions in English football in the 1970s resulted in increased security measures, moves that were to have deadly consequences in 1989. Concerns over player safety saw new security standards put in place in 1974, including high steel fencing separating the masses on the terraces from the pitch.

Hillsborough Stadium, home of Sheffield Wednesday, was often used by England's Football Association for semi-finals of the prestigious FA Cup, which had to be played at neutral venues. The FA favoured the ground, which became the scene of a major problem in 1981 that saw nearly 40 fans hospitalised following a crowd crush, many with broken arms and legs. Despite this and other alarming scenes, the 1989 semi-final between Liverpool and Nottingham Forest on 15 April was scheduled for Hillsborough. Fans were segregated at opposite ends of the ground in a bid to minimise crowd violence, with Liverpool fans herded through a limited number of turnstiles at the Leppings Lane stand at the western end of the ground, behind the goalposts. A massive crowd milled on game day, with media warning fans without tickets not to attend. There was a massive late surge of fans towards the turnstiles just before 3pm and a police constable's request to delay kickoff to allow fans to enter the ground in an orderly fashion was not heeded.

THE SCANDAL

Sensing a crush as 5,000 fans outside the stadium attempted to make a late entry, police opened an exit gate to relieve pressure. That enabled the late fans to charge into the stadium.

But the surge of fans into two already overcrowded pens created massive pressure, as people crammed for a view of the action. Most fans, unaware of the crush of supporters in the front of the main pen, continued to flow in. Many present, except those directly affected, did not realise the problems and were engrossed in the match. But at 3.06pm, on the advice of police, referee Ray Lewis stopped the game as fans, panicking to escape the crush, began climbing the high fences. Other desperate fans managed to open a small gate in the fence, forcing their way through it. Fans high in the West Stand, above the overcrowded Leppings Lane terrace, realised the unfolding disaster and hoisted some fans to safety. Eventually, the pressure created by the overcrowding saw the crush barriers on the terraces break down. Many fans died from suffocation as they stood, such was the pressure created by the thousands of tightly packed people. Some uninjured supporters administered CPR to the dying, while more fans ripped down advertising signs, using them as stretchers to cart away the dying. Some police were still intent on keeping the Liverpool fans segregated, forming a wall on the pitch to keep them away from the Nottingham Forest fans. Over 40 ambulances rushed to the stadium, but police allegedly prevented some from entering the stadium.

THE AFTERMATH

In all, 96 people died, ranging in ages from 10 to 67, while a further 766 were injured, around half of whom required hospitalisation. Of the 96 who died, only 14 made it to hospital for treatment. Among the dead was 10-year-old Jon-Paul Gilhooley, whose cousin Steven Gerrard went on to become Liverpool captain.

The world was shocked by television images of the disaster, with the Queen, Pope John Paul II, US President George H.W. Bush and a host of other dignitaries sending their condolences. The day after the disaster, British Prime Minister Margaret Thatcher toured the scene of the carnage. Liverpool opened its home ground, Anfield Stadium, to allow fans to pay their respects, with an estimated 200,000 filing in over the following days. Hundreds of thousands of pounds poured in to a disaster relief fund for families of the victims.

The government commissioned Lord Justice Taylor to conduct an inquiry. The Taylor Report cited aspects of the police crowd control and the poor facilities at Hillsborough as major factors in the disaster. Another inquiry was held in 2012, absolving Liverpool fans, whom some had attempted to blame for the catastrophe. The disaster became a wake-up call for other antiquated football stadiums in England. Many eliminated terraces altogether, switching to all-seat venues, while perimeter fences were removed. The 10 and 20-year anniversaries of the tragedy were marked by special services at Anfield, which drew massive crowds to mourn the country's worst sporting disaster.

BEN JOHNSON DRUGS SCANDAL, 1988

THE BACKGROUND

Ben Johnson was born in Jamaica in 1961, but emigrated to Canada when he was just 15. There, he showed promise as a runner at the Scarborough Optimists track and field club in Ontario. At the club, Johnson linked up with coach Charlie Francis, a three-time Canadian sprint champion in the early 1970s. A former Canadian national sprint coach, Francis was quick to recognise Johnson's potential, and under his guidance, the powerhouse Johnson exploded onto the world scene at the 1982 Commonwealth Games in Australia, winning two silver medals. Two years later at the Los Angeles Olympics, he took out the bronze in the 100 metres, as well as another bronze in the relay.

Johnson and Carl Lewis, who took the gold, became archrivals, and in 1985, Johnson scored his first win over the American after eight losses. Johnson was made a Member of the Order of Canada in 1987 and later that year beat Lewis to win the World Championship, setting a new world record of 9.83 seconds in the process. At the time, Lewis said, "There are a lot of people coming out of nowhere ... I don't think they are doing it without drugs." Johnson fired back, "When Carl Lewis was winning everywhere, I never said a word against him. And when the next guy comes along and beats me, I won't complain about that either."

The scene was set for an explosive showdown at the 1988 Olympics, where Johnson again proved too good, taking gold and lowering his world record to 9.79 seconds. He became a national hero in Canada yet again.

THE SCANDAL

Three days after his triumph, Johnson was disqualified, after traces of the banned drug stanozolol were found in his urine sample. Canadians were stunned as their pin-up boy became the first athlete in Olympic history to be stripped of a gold medal for drug abuse. He was also stripped of his 1987 world record by the International Association of Athletics Federations.

Johnson initially denied taking drugs, but told a special commission set up by the Canadian government the following year, the Dubin Inquiry, that he had lied at the Olympics. The inquiry lasted three months and heard testimony from over 100 witnesses, including athletes, coaches, doctors and officials. Johnson's coach Francis defended him, declaring he had only used drugs to keep up with rival runners, who he claimed were also on performance-enhancers. Francis later admitted that Johnson used anabolic steroids during his career, but that he did not use stanozolol because it did not agree with his body.

After Johnson was disqualified, his nemesis Lewis was awarded the Olympic gold medal. Lewis' time of 9.92 seconds became the new world record, standing for almost three years. Johnson was given an automatic two-year ban, after which he resumed running.

THE AFTERMATH

Johnson failed to qualify for the 1991 World Championships but made the Canadian squad for the 1992 Olympics. He reached the 100 metres semi-final in Barcelona, but finished in last place after a stumbling start. He won a 50 metres sprint in France in early 1993 in just 5.65 seconds, but was then found guilty of a second doping offence at Montreal and banned for life by the IAAF. Six years later, a Canadian adjudicator allowed Johnson to appeal the ruling on the grounds there were procedural errors in his sentence six years earlier. He entered a track meet in Ontario soon afterwards, but ran alone, posting a time of 11.0 seconds.

Later in 1999, he failed a third drug test, this time for hydrochlorothiazide, a banned diuretic. Johnson was then hired to be personal fitness trainer for the son of now-deceased Libyan dictator Muammar Gaddafi, a budding soccer star. Soccer legend Diego Maradona also employed Johnson as a fitness coach, later describing the sprinter as "the fastest man on earth, whatever anyone says".

Johnson wrote his life story *Seoul to Soul* in 2010, claiming many of the athletes on the world tour in the 1980s were on drugs. He also alleged that someone spiked his drink before his positive drug test in Seoul in 1988, which changed his life forever.

FIGURE-SKATING VOTE TRADE, 2002

THE BACKGROUND

The figure skating pairs competition shaped as one of the highlights of the 2002 Winter Olympics, a showdown between the Russian superstars Elena Berezhnaya and Anton Sikharulidze and their Canadian counterparts Jamie Sale and David Pelletier. And when the skating began in Salt Lake City, the battle did not disappoint. In the free skate, the Russians made a blatant technical error that cost them points, while the Canadians, performing a less difficult routine, did it flawlessly. In the long program, the Canadians performed 'Love Story', their trademark routine and one they had performed extremely well in previous competitions, and again handed in a near-perfect performance. They received excellent marks from most of the nine judges, varying from 5.8 to 5.9 for technical merit. The Canadians needed five scores of 5.9 in presentation to overtake the Russians and win gold, but fell just short, scoring four 5.9s.

The Russians took the gold medal, despite many experts believing they had been out-skated by their rivals, a decision that angered the pro-Canadian crowd and was blasted on live TV by US and Canadian official commentary teams. There were whispers of bias – the Russian, Chinese, Polish, Ukrainian and French judges placed the Russians first, while the American, Canadian, German and Japanese judges went with the Canadians. But allegations of bias were common in Olympic competition and that seemed the end of the matter.

THE SCANDAL

Officials became sceptical about the scores handed in by the French judge, Marie-Reine Le

Gougne. She was confronted by officials after the event, who alleged that she broke down, admitting she had been pressured by French officials to ensure the Russians won. She was alleged to have said that she was told to do it, so the Russians could repay the favour for the French in the ice dance voting a few days later. But shortly after this was reported, Le Gougne denied she had made any such statements and that she stood by her vote, believing the Russians deserved to win.

The controversy created an international scandal, with the Russians dismissing it as 'sore losing'. They pointed out that, in a previous year's world championships, the Canadian Sale fell while performing a triple-toe loop and made a mistake in her execution of the double axel, but the Canadians won anyway; there had been no controversy or investigation then.

Nonetheless, the International Skating Union held a press conference the day after the competition, declaring it would carry out an internal investigation into the judging process. It emerged that event referee Ron Pfenning, an American, had filed an official complaint about the judging process. Days later, after intense media and public pressure, the ISU and IOC president Jacques Rogge announced that they would upgrade Sale and Pelletier's medal from silver to gold. The Russian pair, Berezhnaya and Sikharulidze, would keep their gold as well, as they did nothing wrong and were not involved in the judging farce. Organisers held a second medal ceremony at which the Russians again received gold medals, but the Chinese duo that took bronze, Shen Xue and Zhao Hongbo, did not attend.

THE AFTERMATH

In April 2002, the ISU found Marie-Reine Le Gougne guilty of misconduct, banning her for three years. The president of French skating, Didier Gailhaguet, was also ousted for three years. Both were barred from the 2006 Winter Olympics. "We went through the papers, we went through the evidence and then we decided," ISU president Ottavio Cinquanta said after a five-hour meeting. "We are more than confident we took the right decision."

Le Gougne slammed the hearing, claiming she was railroaded by the ISU. "It was a masquerade," Le Gougne said. "It is scandalous. My most basic rights of defence were denied. They have decapitated me from the start." She threatened to tip the bucket in the ISU over the way the sport was run. "They won't stop me now … I have nothing more to lose. I will fight this to the end."

The ISU also changed the way it adjudicated contests in the wake of the scandal, bringing in a new "secret judging" system by which judges' marks are posted anonymously.

The Russians remained convinced that the revision of the medals and changes to the judging system were unnecessary, believing it had taken the gloss off Russia's gold medal.

"It's a disgraceful fuss," Deputy Prime Minister Valentina Matviyenko said. "The International Olympic Committee should get to the root of it and not allow American mass media and amateurs to give marks to our skaters."

DIS-ONISCHENKO, THE KGB OLYMPIC CHEAT, 1976

THE BACKGROUND

Boris Onischenko was a Russian hero in 1976. He was one of the world's finest fencers, a star of the Soviet Union's modern pentathlon team ... and a colonel in the dreaded KGB. Four years earlier, the imposing athlete from the Ukraine won the individual gold medal and helped the Russians to a team silver medal at the Munich Olympics. His biggest rival on the Great Britain team was a British Army officer, Jim Fox. When these two old adversaries came face to face at the Montreal Olympics, it created an international drama of Cold War proportions that newspapers around the world milked for all it was worth.

The pentathlon is a gruelling test of strength and stamina in pistol shooting, fencing, 200m freestyle swimming, show jumping and a 3km cross-country run. In his first round of the fencing, Fox noticed that Onischenko scored hits almost at will, even when it seemed he had not hit his opponent. Fox came up against Onischenko in the second round. When Onischenko attacked him for the first time, the Brit, highly suspicious of his rival, leaned back far further than he normally would. Despite a clear miss, the light came on, indicating a 'hit'.

THE SCANDAL

Fox immediately protested, but at that stage everyone merely suspected a mechanical malfunction. Onischenko continued to compete with a replacement weapon, and ironically still beat Fox, winning eight of his nine bouts in the session, many easily. At one stage of a tense morning, as the two passed, Onischenko said to Fox, "Jim, I am very sorry", words that puzzled Fox at the time, but that would become very clear only hours later.

Meanwhile, officials sent the weapon off for testing. It was there they discovered Onischenko had 'hot-wired' his épée so that with a gentle push of his thumb on the handle, a 'hit' would be registered. Within the hour, officials had kicked him out of the Games and the entire Soviet modern pentathlon team was disqualified as a result. Onischenko was quickly hustled out of the village and back to Russia. At first, athletes from behind the Iron Curtain were rallied alongside the fencer, convinced he had been framed. The Eastern Bloc countries were rumoured to be on the verge of quitting the Games, before the truth was fully revealed.

Fox, who had been a friendly rival of Onischenko's for many years, was clearly rattled by the drama. He struggled for the rest of the competition, going disastrously in one of his strongest events, the pistol, as Britain slipped to eighth spot on the leaderboard. On the fourth day, he regained his composure in the swimming, moving the Brits up to fifth. It all came down to the cross-country on the final day, where Fox ran the anchor leg. The veteran of the team at 36, Fox ran the race of his life. He was so distressed that he needed oxygen after collapsing on the finish line. But he had done it. After half an hour of mathematical calculations – there were no computers then – officials declared Great Britain had won the gold medal for the pentathlon, snatching it with Fox's late surge from Czechoslovakia.

THE AFTERMATH

The win only served to create more animosity among the disqualified Soviet team. "We weren't bosom pals, but we'd often get drunk on vodka together in the evenings at various competitions," Fox reflected years later. "So there was a relationship between Boris and me." Upon hearing of his blatant attempts to win gold by cheating, Russian athletes eventually lost all sympathy for Onischenko, with several members of the volleyball team declaring they would throw him out of the team's hotel window if they saw him. He made front-page news throughout the world, dubbed 'DIS-ONISCHENKO' by the world's media.

The disgraced Onischenko was never seen or heard of outside the USSR again. Legend has it he was sent off to a salt mine in Siberia, but such reports are more than likely an exaggeration. Fox remains a British national hero and was awarded an OBE in the Queen's Birthday Honours List in 2010. He now lives in retirement in the British countryside, where he is battling Parkinson's disease.

GREEK STARS KICKED OUT OF GAMES, 2004

THE BACKGROUND

Ekaterini Thanou and Konstandinos Kenderis were the pride of Greece leading up to the country hosting the 2004 Olympics. Sprinter Kenderis had won a gold medal in the Sydney Olympics in 2000 in the 200 metres dash and backed that up with further victories in the 2001 World Athletics Championships and 2002 European Championships. Thanou, also a sprinter, won silver in the 100 metres dash at the Sydney Olympics behind Marion Jones, and in the 2001 World Championships. She took gold in the 2002 European Championship and was considered a great chance to win gold for the home country at the 2004 Olympics.

But the day before the Athens Olympics opening ceremony, the pair, who were training partners, failed to turn up at a scheduled drug test. That night, they went to a local hospital in Athens, claiming they had been injured in a motorcycle accident. Thanou and Kenderis told officials they suffered sprains and minor injuries when they lost control of the motorcycle. They claimed an unidentified man drove them 18 miles to the emergency ward of an Athens hospital where they were assessed and said to be in a stable condition.

The pair spent several days in hospital and the Greek people went into mourning, stunned that two of their best gold medal prospects were now out of the Games as the result of this freak accident.

THE SCANDAL

After holding an internal investigation, Greek officials suspended the pair from competing at the Games. It was the third time they had missed mandatory drug tests. The pair hired lawyers, who vowed to fight any attempt to remove them from the Games. Officials also expressed doubts about the accident, with allegations emerging that it had been staged so that the pair would not have to undergo drug testing. Among other evidence, a kiosk owner at the site of the accident told Greek reporters he did not see or hear anything when the accident was alleged to have occurred.

Members of the Hellenic Olympic Committee voted 5-1 to remove Thanou and Kenderis from the team, in a move that shocked the nation. They also faced possible sanctions from the International Olympic Committee for missing the drug tests. The two faced an IOC Disciplinary Commission hearing, after which they announced they were pulling out of the Olympics "in the best interests of the country".

In 2005, the Greek Track and Field Federation cleared the pair of deliberately evading the drug tests, ruling that they had not been properly notified prior to the tests. The International Association of Athletics Federations attempted to overturn the Greek ruling and ban the duo for a minimum of two years. The pair sat out for two years while debate raged about their status. But in 2006, on the day the duo were set to appeal their bans in the Court of Arbitration of Sport, they dropped their appeals, in a move that surprised the IAAF. "The proceedings are now at an end," the IAAF said in a statement.

But the matter wasn't over – the pair still faced charges of making false statements to police in regards to the motorcycle crash.

THE AFTERMATH

Kenteris retired after serving his two-year ban, but Thanou returned to big-time competition at the 2007 European Indoor Athletics Championships in the English city of Birmingham. She won her heat in the 60 metres sprint, despite some heckling from the crowd, but could only manage sixth place in the final.

The same year Marion Jones, who had beaten Thanou for the gold medal in Sydney seven years earlier, admitted she had taken performance-enhancing drugs and was stripped of her gold from Sydney. Under normal circumstances, Thanou would have been in line to receive the gold in her place, but the IOC decided against upgrading her silver. Thanou was then chosen by Greece for the 2008 Olympics, but the executive board of the IOC banned her from competing in Beijing.

The pair believed they were victimised by the IOC in the wake of the Athens scandal. "This is discrimination against Thanou," her lawyer Nikos Kollias said. "Athletes who have admitted taking performance-enhancing drugs and were punished are taking part in the Beijing Games without problem."

In 2011, Kenteris and Thanou were found guilty of perjury over the staged motorcycle crash and each given 31-month suspended jail sentences. Their coach, Christos Tzekos, was given a 33-month jail term. But four months later, the pair won their appeal and were acquitted of the charges. Tzekos' verdict on a charge of possession and storage of illegal substances was upheld, but he was acquitted of perjury; his 33-month sentence was reduced to 12 months, suspended for three years.

"This is a vindication that we have been talking about and fighting for – for seven years," said Thanou's lawyer, Maria Kevga.

COLLEGE BASKETBALL POINT SHAVING, 1951

THE BACKGROUND

City College of New York was the talk of the sports world in the United States in 1950, for all the right reasons. The college won the National Invitation and NCAA Mens Division I basketball tournaments, becoming the first team to win both. Along the way, they scored upset wins over more fancied teams from bigger and richer colleges on the west coast and the game's strong schools in the Midwest.

The Beavers, as they were known, started the year as rank outsiders, but by the end of that memorable season were recognised as the best college team in the land. Coached by Nat Holman, they beat Bradley 71-68, in a tense final game. The team produced several stars – the likes of Al Roth, Ed Warner, Ed Roman and Herb Cohen – and NBA clubs were lining up to sign the team's star talent.

Only a few years earlier, in 1945, authorities were concerned at the big money being wagered on sport and the potential implications for organised crime. They passed a new bill, section 382 of the penal code, establishing as illegal any attempt to bribe players in sporting events, irrespective of whether the games were amateur or professional.

THE SCANDAL

There were no suspicions about the Beavers, or other college basketball teams, until January 1951, when New York District Attorney Frank Hogan began a secret investigation. On 17 January, Hogan swooped. Police arrested two Manhattan players, Henry Poppe and Jack Byrnes, as well as three bookmakers, brothers Ben and Irving Schwartzenberg, and Cornelius Kelleher. The scandal hit the newspapers as Hogan booked his suspects on bribery and conspiracy charges, and for violating section 382.

It was found that Poppe and Byrnes had been involved with the bookies in 1949–50, receiving $50 a week, plus $3,000 to ensure Manhattan lost games by required points margins. In February, as City College returned from a road trip to Philadelphia, police arrested star players Warner, Roman and Roth at New York's Penn Station. And that was just the start – Hogan eventually arrested 32 players in all, from seven colleges across the country. Several bookmakers and 'fixers' were also arrested. Included in the swoop were several Long Island University players, and the scandal became so large that LIU's game against Cincinnati, scheduled for Madison Square Garden, was called off. The arrests continued, with three more CCNY players implicated in March.

In July, five Bradley players admitted taking bribes from gamblers to reduce their scoring in a game against Oregon State and St Joseph's. In October, three Bradley players, Gene Melchiorre, Bill Mann and George Chianakos, pleaded guilty to a misdemeanour in a New York court. They could have been jailed, but the judge praised them for their cooperation and hinted at a suspended sentence. In October, three Kentucky players were arrested for taking $500 bribes for point shaving. Jack Molinas, who played for Detroit in the NBA in 1953, was suspended for gambling and found to have bet on his former college, Columbia University, in 1951.

THE AFTERMATH

Several of the players received jail terms, while others got off with suspended sentences. Kentucky's All American Bill Spivey was barred from playing for the team and attending the university in 1952; Spivey was allegedly accused of involvement by team-mates, but never directly implicated. He was subsequently refused entry to the NBA and sued for $800,000, receiving an out-of-court settlement of $10,000. The NCAA suspended the entire Kentucky basketball program for 1952–53, despite legendary coach Adolph Rupp's earlier claims that "they [the match-fixers] couldn't reach my boys with a ten-foot pole".

When it came to City College, apparently the worst offender among the teams, Warner was jailed for six months and banned from ever playing in the NBA. He was jailed again in the 1960s for drugs charges before becoming a high school basketball referee. Roman received a suspended sentence, but was also banned from the NBA for life. Roth received a six-month term in a workhouse, but his sentence was suspended when he joined the army. Holman was cleared of any involvement or knowledge of the scandal and continued to coach CCNY until retiring in 1960 after 37 seasons.

Stunned by the magnitude of the deceit, NCAA officials believed playing games in New York, where several mobsters operated, was a recipe for disaster, so avoided the Big Apple for major games as much as possible for the next three decades. Meanwhile, big-time betting continues to thrive on college basketball.

'DOLLY' TACKLES APARTHEID, 1968

THE BACKGROUND

Born in Cape Town in 1931, of Indian and Portugese descent, Basil D'Oliveira was classed as 'coloured' by South Africa's Apartheid government. A fine cricketer in his youth, D'Oliveira was a solid batsman and handy change bowler. He played for South Africa's national 'non-white' team, but longed to prove himself at the highest level of the game, in Test cricket. South Africa began playing cricket in 1889, only selecting white players despite the impressive credentials of hundreds of coloured cricketers down the years. They also only played against 'white' countries – New Zealand, Australia and England – refusing to compete against powerful cricket nations India, Pakistan and the West Indies on racial grounds.

Realising he would never achieve his dream of playing for his country, D'Oliveira emigrated to England at the age of 29, in 1960. He became a British citizen and played for Worcestershire. After proving himself in county cricket, he was selected for his Test debut for England in 1966, performing solidly against the West Indies. Later that year he hit his first Test century, a fine 109 against India. He followed that up with half-centuries in both innings of the First Test against Pakistan and was named one of cricket bible *Wisden*'s players of the year.

In 1968, he was in line for selection to tour his native country in a test of Apartheid that would reverberate around the globe. Politicians in South Africa rallied against D'Oliveira's proposed selection, saying the MCC was "wasting their time" and that South Africa would not be held to "political blackmail". New Zealand rugby officials, meanwhile, asked for clarification of whether native Maoris would be allowed into South Africa on their proposed tour. After some deliberation, South African officials declared they would be welcomed if chosen by New Zealand.

THE SCANDAL

South African Prime Minister John Vorster, desperate for the apartheid issue to be kept out of the international spotlight, warned the Marylebone Cricket Club (MCC), which ran the game in England, that D'Oliveira was not welcome in South Africa. Human rights campaigners demanded that D'Oliveira be selected, because his form warranted a place on the tour and the colour of his skin was irrelevant. "We are not prepared to receive a team thrust upon us by people whose interests are not in the game but to gain certain political objectives which they do not even attempt to hide," Vorster said in return. "The MCC team is not the team of the MCC, but of the anti-apartheid movement." English sports minister Denis Howell described Vorster's statement as "ludicrous", and the MCC hit back too, telling Vorster the tour could not go ahead if South Africa made "preconditions about selection".

D'Oliveira was originally omitted from the team – some say for poor form, others insist for political reasons. When an English official declared his form did not warrant selection, *The Guardian* newspaper ran an editorial stating that "anyone who would swallow that would believe the moon was a currant bun". But when one player, Tom Cartwright, withdrew from the team through injury, D'Oliveira gained selection in his place. An anonymous letter to the MCC threatened to blow up the tourists' plane if D'Oliveira was on it. The MCC met with South African cricket officials in London and, with neither side willing to budge on the issue, the tour was called off.

THE AFTERMATH

A spokesman for South African cricket (SACA) released a statement declaring D'Oliveira was "not acceptable for reasons beyond the control of SACA. We are terribly sorry and disappointed." With the affair exposing South Africa's racist policies, the international community became united in its opposition to apartheid. South Africa was all but excluded from world sport for the next two decades, until being re-admitted after the end of apartheid in 1991.

A quiet, shy man, D'Oliveira became a reluctant hero throughout the sporting world. In the year 2000, he was voted among the 10 South African cricketers of the century, despite never playing for his country. He was treated like a favourite son when presented to the crowd at the Newlands Ground in his hometown of Cape Town. At age 69, it was the first time he had ever been legally allowed to step foot onto the arena. D'Oliveira's son Damien also played cricket for Worcestershire, while his grandson Brett D'Oliveira made his debut for the same county in 2011.

Basil D'Oliveira died in England in 2011, aged 80. The prize for the winner of the Test series between England and South Africa is now known as the Basil D'Oliveira Trophy.

WARNE'S DIET PILL BAN, 2003

THE BACKGROUND

Shane Warne was the most famous cricketer of the modern era, a brilliant spin bowler known throughout the game for his ability to win matches and his sometimes-outlandish behaviour off the field.

Born in the Australian state of Victoria in 1969, Warne reinvented the lost art of leg spin bowling and changed the way the game was played. After bursting onto the international scene in 1992, Warne took more than 1,000 wickets in Test and one-day international cricket. Only Sri Lankan wizard Muttiah Muralitharan has taken more. Warne guided Australia to many famous Test wins and in 2000 was voted one of five Wisden Cricketers of the Century, the only bowler in the group. Warne was also a handy batsman, who scored more than 3,000 Test runs. His highest score was 99 and he holds the curious record of most runs in Test cricket history without having scored a century.

Warne's life away from cricket attracted nearly as many headlines as his exploits with the ball. Among other colourful incidents, he had an on-again, off-again relationship with wife Simone after being caught sending text messages to other women, and played professional poker for big money on TV. Tabloid newspapers almost went into meltdown when Warne began dating model Elizabeth Hurley in 2010, with the pair subsequently announcing their engagement.

THE SCANDAL

On the day the 2003 World Cup in South Africa was due to begin, Warne was sent back to

Australia when it was revealed he had failed a drug test for a game in Sydney in January, testing positive to a banned diuretic compound. Warne admitted he had taken the diuretic, but claimed it was a pill given to him by his mother to help him lose weight. He denied any knowledge that the pill was on the banned list. While diuretics are used mainly to lose weight – Warne had shed 14 kilos in the previous 12 months – they can also mask performance-enhancing drugs.

"I was shocked and absolutely devastated to be informed by ASDA (Australian Sports Drug Agency) yesterday that a test sample which was collected in Australia on the 22nd of January indicated the presence of a prohibited substance," Warne said. The news made headlines around the world and stunned the Australian camp, less than an hour before the team, trying to defend its World Cup title, would play the first game of the tournament against Pakistan. Warne faced the prospect of a two-year ban under the International Cricket Council's strict drug guidelines, leading to speculation that, at 33, his career could be over.

World Anti-Doping Agency chairman Dick Pound slammed Warne's defence and called for a two-year ban. "The source is not relevant, the responsibility of an athlete is to not take prohibited substances," Pound said. "You cannot have an IQ over room temperature and be unaware of this as an international athlete. This is original: 'My mum gave it to me.'"

THE AFTERMATH

After a lengthy hearing and much debate, the Australian Cricket Board Anti-Doping Committee suspended Warne from all cricket for 12 months, effective from 10 February 2003. In an eight-hour hearing, the Committee was not moved by Warne's defence that his mother gave him the diuretics hydrochlorothiazide and amiloride and ruled that there were no exceptional circumstances to justify dismissal of the charge. Mrs Brigitte Warne gave evidence at the hearing, confirming her son's original story.

The committee decided that there was no performance-enhancing effect in the diuretic, and, given that there was no evidence of anabolic steroids and that Warne had shown full cooperation, they would impose a lighter sentence than the usual two-year ban. "We hope that the extraordinary publicity about this unfortunate incident at least helps reinforce to all cricketers that doping practices are unacceptable, and that athletes should always check before taking any medication," ACB boss James Sutherland said.

Later that year, in August, Warne was allowed to play in charity games, a move that was criticised by WADA. "It is bizarre," WADA chief executive David Howman said. "A ban means not participating in any form. It is not a ban if he is training or playing – a ban means not participating in any form. I find this ruling particularly bizarre because it is out of character with Australia's strong anti-doping stance."

Warne returned to top-flight cricket in February 2004 and only a month later became the first spin bowler to take 500 Test wickets. He continued to play Test cricket until retiring in 2007 and after that starred in the Indian Premier League, continuing to take wickets and thrill crowds.

MARION JONES DRUG DISGRACE, 2007

THE BACKGROUND

Born in Los Angeles in 1975 to an African-American father and Belizean mother, Marion Jones was a star teenage athlete and basketballer. She attended the University of North Carolina and began dating a track coach and shot putter, C. J. Hunter. Because of rules against coaches dating athletes, Hunter resigned from UNC and the pair were married in October, 1998.

Marion Jones on the track in 2006.

They prepared for the Sydney Olympics under coach Trevor Graham and in the lead-up to the 2000 Games, Jones declared she was chasing five gold medals. Hunter, meanwhile, dropped out of the shot put, citing a knee injury, but said he would travel to Sydney to support his wife. In Sydney, Jones won gold as planned in her first event, but on the same day the IOC revealed that Hunter had failed four tests for the banned substance nandrolone, an anabolic steroid. With Jones sitting stoically by his side, Hunter gave a tearful statement, saying he had never taken performance-enhancing drugs. The pharmaceutical manufacturer BALCO, which had been supplying Jones, Hunter and other athletes with "nutritional supplements", said the test results were an error caused by an iron supplement.

Jones herself was used to drug allegations – she had been accused several times, going back to her college days, of illicit use, but had never tested positive. At Sydney she finished with three gold and two bronze medals, and became the pin-up girl of the 2000 Olympics.

THE SCANDAL

In a US television interview in late 2004, the founder of BALCO, Victor Conte, alleged he had given Jones a cocktail of illegal drugs before and during the Sydney Olympics. Hunter, who had divorced Jones in 2002, added fuel to the fire, telling reporters he had seen Jones inject herself in the abdomen with steroids. But with Jones insisting she had never failed a drug test, there was insufficient evidence to bring charges, until several years later.

In June of 2006, *The Washington Post* reported that Jones' A sample from the USA Track and Field Championships in Indianapolis had tested positive to erythropoietin, or EPO, a performance-enhancing drug on the banned list. Jones hired high-profile lawyer Howard Jacobs, who declared in September 2006 that her B sample had come back negative, clearing her. But in October 2007, Jones finally confessed all. She admitted that she had used steroids prior to the Sydney Olympics and also pleaded guilty to lying to federal agents while under oath. She told a US District Court in New York that she had made false statements regarding BALCO. Jones then held a press conference, publicly admitting she was a drug cheat. In tears, she declared, "It is with a great amount of shame … I stand before you and tell you I have betrayed your trust … and you have the right to be angry with me … I have let my country down and I have let myself down."

THE AFTERMATH

Adding to her problems was a cheque fraud drama, in which a cheque worth $25,000 was allegedly deposited into her bank account as part of a multi-million dollar scheme. Jones ended up pleading guilty to making false statements about the scheme to the US Department of Homeland Security. In January 2008, Jones accepted a plea agreement and received a six-month jail sentence. Judge Kenneth Karas slammed Jones' integrity after sentencing, declaring her actions were "not a one-off mistake … but a repetition in an attempt to break the law." The sentence was the maximum allowed and Jones accepted it. "I respect the judge's order and

I truly hope people will learn from my mistakes," she said.

The US Anti-Doping Agency insisted that all the records she'd set from September 2000 onwards be struck from the books and that she return all medals and prizes. The US Olympic Committee also weighed in, with Chairman Peter Ueberroth declaring her confession "long overdue and underscores the shame and dishonour that are inherent with cheating". In October 2008, Jones returned the five medals she won in Sydney. Ueberroth added that her team-mates' relay medals should also be returned and his stance was backed by the IOC, but this decision was overturned in 2010. Jones didn't just lose her medals, she lost sponsors, and experienced massive financial problems as a result.

After she had confessed her guilt and returned her medals, Ueberroth and the USOC board wrote an official letter of apology to the 205 nations that competed in the Sydney Olympics and also apologised to the people of Australia, who had so willingly declared Jones a world champion. Jones re-invented herself after serving her time in jail, lecturing young athletes on the importance of avoiding drugs. In 2010, she won a contract in the Women's National Basketball Association with the Tulsa Shock.

HANSIE CRONJE'S CRICKET FIXING, 2000

THE BACKGROUND

Hansie Cronje came from a proud South African cricketing family. His father Ewie played first class cricket for Orange Free State in the 1960s and his older brother Frans also played at the top level. Johannes 'Hansie' Cronje was born in Bloemfontein in 1969 and excelled in many sports in his youth, most notably rugby union and cricket. He was selected in both sports for Orange Free State at schoolboy level. He made his first-class cricket debut in 1988 at the age of 18 and quickly established himself as a regular in the Currie Cup with his elegant strokeplay and ability to accumulate large scores.

At 21, he was named captain of Orange Free State and led them to victory in both the Castle Cup and Total Power Series in 1992–93. He won national honours in 1992, representing South Africa in the World Cup. Test selection soon followed and Cronje proved himself to be a world-class batsman.

On the 1993–94 tour of Australia, skipper Kepler Wessels was injured and Cronje was named to take over the captaincy. He did a good job under challenging circumstances in Australia and was named permanent captain of his country in 1994–95, leading South Africa to some memorable wins in the ensuing years.

THE SCANDAL

In April 2000, Indian police announced they had recorded secret conversations between Cronje and a leading Indian betting figure, Sanjay Chawla, regarding match-fixing. The following day, Cronje issued an angry denial. But the South African Cricket Board (UCBSA) sacked Cronje as captain three days later after he confessed he accepted a sum of money, said to be around US$15,000, for predicting results in a recent series of limited overs internationals against India. Cronje still insisted he did not actually fix results.

Two months later, a special commission was set up to investigate the affair. Gibbs alleged that Cronje had offered him $15,000 to score less than 20 runs in the match against India in Nagpur. Ironically, Gibbs scored 74 runs and didn't receive a cent. Cronje then took the stand, and the cricket world was rocked as he read a 45-minute statement that would change his life forever.

Cronje revealed his long association with bookmakers, which went back to 1996, when former Indian captain Mohammad Azharuddin introduced him to businessman and alleged bookmaker Mukesh Gupta. Cronje admitted Gupta paid him $30,000 to influence South Africa to lose the third Test against India in Kanpur. Cronje had already been dismissed and said he did not convey the offer to his team-mates, and the South Africans lost the match anyway. He alleged he did nothing, but still got the money. He added that he received a further $50,000 from Gupta for information about the Proteas team and match conditions.

The money increased – at one stage Cronje allegedly received $200,000. By then he was passing on regular team information, including the scores on which he intended to declare his innings closed. He was offered $300,000 to lose the third Test against India, but refused. During the fifth Test against England in 2000, a bookmaker had offered Cronje R500,000 to his charity of choice and a further gift if he made an early declaration. Cronje did, England won, and the bookmaker gave Cronje R50,000 – not the initial amount promised – and a leather jacket.

The money continued to flow for several years.

THE AFTERMATH

In October, UCBSA banned Cronje for life. He appealed against his life ban the following year to the South African High Court, and lost.

In June 2002, Cronje was the only passenger flying in a light aircraft in South Africa's Western Cape during a storm. The plane, a Hawker Siddeley HS 748, was unable to land and circled the airport in treacherous conditions. It crashed into the Outeniqua Mountains near the airport during the storm, killing the two pilots and Cronje instantly. Cronje was just 32.

The South African High Court held an inquest into the crash four years later, putting the accident down to pilot error. Conspiracy theorists believe foul play could have been involved, and their theories gained more interest following the death of Pakistan coach Bob Woolmer in suspicious circumstances in 2007.

In 2004, Hansie Cronje was voted by the public as the eleventh-greatest South African ever in a television series called *Great South Africans*, despite having finished his career in disgrace.

EAST GERMAN UNWITTING DOPER'S SEX CHANGE, 1997

THE BACKGROUND

East Germany was among the pioneers of doping in sport in the 1960s and 1970s. The country's communist regime was known to have conducted a systematic and ruthless program of performance-enhancing drugs, closing itself off from much of the sporting world as its scientists enjoyed a free rein. Many times, the athletes themselves had no idea they were being doped, with officials keeping them in the dark as huge amounts of steroids were pumped into their systems. Some were as young as 10 years old.

In the 1970s, as drug testing began to be introduced in many major sporting events, East German officials tested their athletes 'in house' before they left the country. Those who tested positive were stood down, with injury usually cited as the reason. Officials kept much of this secret, but word got out, mainly through athletes who defected to the West.

While the heartbreaking stories of many of these athletes has still never been told, Andreas Krieger is an exception. Born in Berlin in 1966 as Heidi Krieger, she was identified early on as a potential star and, without her knowledge, put on massive doses of anabolic steroids. Krieger won the gold medal in shot put at the 1986 European Athletics Championships, blowing away the field with a dynamic best of 21.10 metres.

THE SCANDAL

Unknown to her, officials had begun doping Krieger with powerful anabolic steroids when she was around 16. She believed she was taking vitamins. By the age of 18, while she was training and competing, Krieger noticed she was beginning to develop male physical characteristics.

She became the subject of ridicule, called a homosexual and a drag queen when she walked down the street. Once, at Vienna Airport, she asked for directions to the toilet and was pointed towards the men's room.

Historians Werner Franke and Brigitte Berendonk, who studied the East German doping scandal extensively and reported on it in their book *Doping: From Research to Deceit*, believe Krieger was fed nearly 2,600 milligrams of steroids in the year she won the European title. That is almost double the amount allegedly taken by Ben Johnson when he tested positive to drugs at the 1988 Olympics after winning gold.

Krieger retired in 1990 and continued to experience changes in her body. In 1997, she had a sex-change operation, becoming a man and changing her name to Andreas. Telling a psychologist of her plans before the surgery, he asked, "So you want to change from a man to a woman?"

She insists she had no knowledge that she was being doped. "The only thing I could do was sports," Krieger said in an interview years later. "I got to travel, I received recognition. I got the feeling that I belonged. That's what I wanted, to belong. From my point of view, I deserved it. I had worked hard. To question whether these were hormones I was being given, I didn't ask or suspect."

By 1991, the toll on her body was too much, and she retired in great physical pain.

THE AFTERMATH

After the German Democratic Republic was disbanded in 1990 to become part of the Federal Republic of Germany, evidence was found that the Stasi, the dreaded state secret police, were in charge of an organised system of doping throughout the 1970s and 1980s. While many countries employed doping, only in East Germany can it be argued that it was a part of state policy. Estimates put the number of athletes who were part of the doping program to around 10,000. East Germany was a sporting powerhouse at the time, but at a terrible cost to its athletes, many of whom ended up with mental and physical problems in later life.

Several athletes went on to take legal action against the manufacturers of drugs in East Germany, while some officials and coaches have been charged. In 2003–05, a group of former athletes sued the Deutscher Olympischer Sportbund, the successor to the East German Olympic Committee, in a Frankfurt court. Nearly 200 athletes each received amounts between €9,000 and €10,000. Their names were not released under the terms of the agreement, in which they agreed not to seek any further compensation. Andreas Krieger is believed to be one of this group. In constant pain from lifting huge weights while on drugs, he can barely hold down a regular job. Since retirement, Krieger has worked two days a week as a clerk and married East

German swimmer Ute Krause, ironically another victim of the state's systematic doping of its sports stars.

Every year, the German government presents the Heidi Krieger Medal to a person who works to fight doping in sports. The trophy's centrepiece is Krieger's gold medal from the 1986 European Championships.

FOOTBALLER'S THAI PRISON HELL, 1978

THE BACKGROUND

Paul Hayward was a talented all-round sportsman, born in Sydney, Australia, in 1954. Raised in a tough neighborhood in the inner city, Hayward was a handy light welterweight boxer who had two professional bouts, winning both on points. He was spoken of as a possible Olympic fighter, but ruled ineligible under the strict amateur rules of the day because he received money for playing rugby league, his first love; playing for Waterloo Waratahs in South Sydney, he had been given a professional contract by the Newtown club. A cheeky halfback or five-eighth, Hayward made his debut in 1973 and was a regular in the Jets' top side. He was highly regarded as a rugged playmaker and named in a Combined Sydney representative team featuring some of the game's biggest names that toured New Zealand in 1976.

Hayward was the brother-in-law of notorious criminal Arthur 'Neddy' Smith, who was serving a life sentence in a New South Wales prison for a variety of crimes. It was through Smith that Hayward came to know Warren Fellows, a Sydney man who worked a variety of jobs, including as a barman and hairdresser. In the rugby league off-season of 1978, only weeks after the end of the football season, Hayward and Fellows travelled to Thailand, allegedly on holiday.

THE SCANDAL

The pair's true purpose was much more sinister – they apparently planned to traffic illegal drugs back to Australia. Fellows, whose father was a jockey and had won the 1949 Melbourne Cup, allegedly made several successful runs as a 'mule' in previous years, importing large amounts of cocaine and other drugs from South America and Asia, and roped Hayward in with the promise of easy money.

The plan was to put the drugs, which would be heroin, into specially designed hidden compartments in their suitcases and simply walk past Customs officials with the contraband in their luggage. Fellows claimed to have used the suitcase ploy before with great success. While in Bangkok, the pair met local bar owner William Sinclair. But the plan never got off first base, as a 'mole' informed police of the plan. The pair were arrested when a large group of police raided their room at the Montien Hotel in Bangkok. In their possession were 8.4 kilograms of heroin, one of the largest hauls recovered by Thai police for many years. Sinclair was charged, too, even though Fellows has always insisted Sinclair was not in on the operation and had just been in the wrong place at the wrong time.

Fellows had a bad feeling about the plan the day after meeting Sinclair and decided to destroy the heroin the next morning. But after a long night of drinking, he forgot, and he and Hayward were arrested the following morning. Hayward and Fellows each received 30-year sentences, effectively life imprisonment in the brutal Thai jail system. Hayward started his sentence in the Lard Yao prison before being transferred to Bangkwang. Regarded as one of the most brutal prisons in Asia, Bangkwang houses many death row and life-term prisoners. Inmates are shackled with leg irons and receive one bowl of rice per day.

THE AFTERMATH

Back in Sydney, a tearful Gail Hayward poured out her heart to *The Australian Women's Weekly*. "I don't care if he's guilty or not guilty. I want him back ... I'm so used to having him here. I knew where he was when I needed him." The Haywards had two small children at the time, and Gail was pregnant with a third.

Hayward was finally released in April 1989, thanks to a royal pardon from the Thai king. But more than 10 years in the Thai prison system had taken their toll on the once-proud athlete. Hayward began using heroin in jail and contracted HIV-AIDS from using shared needles. He returned to Sydney a shell of a man, struggling to pick up the pieces of his life with Gail and his three children. Hayward spoke little of his time in prison after returning home, but Fellows, who was released the following year, was more open, writing a best-selling book called *The Damage Done*, detailing the pair's experiences. Fellows revealed he had attempted to commit suicide several times, that they were subject to regular beatings, ate rats to survive and were often put in solitary confinement. They also witnessed torture and execution, often going to sleep to the sound of screams in the night. Paul Hayward died of a heroin overdose just three years after his release in 1992, aged only 38.

OLYMPIC RUNNER HITCHES A RIDE, 1904

THE BACKGROUND

Contrary to popular belief, the marathon was not part of the ancient Greek Olympics. The Greek Games mainly had races over short distances, the longest being around 4,800 metres, close to three miles. The marathon was born in 490BC when a message runner named Pheidippides ran the 25 miles from Marathon to Athens to tell Athenians of a famous battle victory. Legend has it Pheidippides told the town "Rejoice, we conquer"... and then dropped dead. To honour Pheidippides, the marathon was held at the first modern Olympics in 1896, starting at Marathon and ending in Athens. Appropriately, a Greek, an unknown shepherd named Spiridon Louis, won the first Olympic marathon in 1896, earning himself a place in his country's folklore.

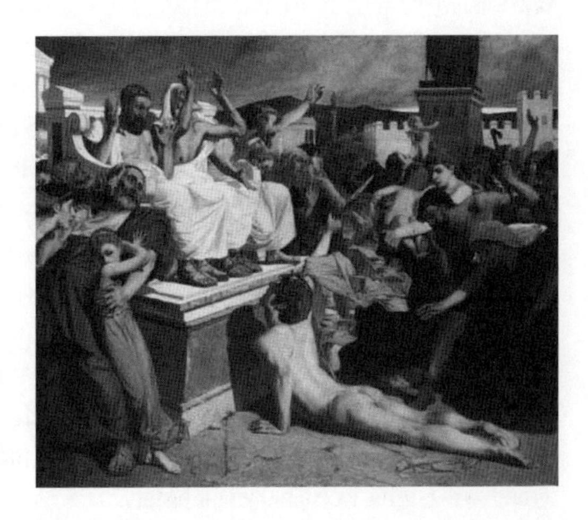

Pheidippides depicted in a painting by Luc-Olivier Merson (1869).

From these obscure beginnings, the marathon became a feature of the Olympic Games, but at St Louis in 1904, it developed into little more than a farce. Officials scheduled the race to begin at 3pm, in stifling heat. Some 31 runners took off from Washington University and were preceded by a convoy of horses and cars containing coaches, police, journalists and officials. As a result, the traffic on the dirt roads created a cloud of dust that made it difficult for the runners to see, let alone breathe. Officials neglected, or simply forgot, to allow for water stops, with just one drink station 12 miles into the race. Several runners were seen breaking from the race to run into fields and orchards in search of fruit to quench their thirst. One runner was chased by a farmer's wild dogs as he ran through the fields. Yet another runner passed out by the side of the road, and was found by concerned onlookers in a state "near death". Historians called the race a "circus", with noted Olympic writer David Wallechinsky saying, "The 1904 Marathon ranks very high on the list of bizarre events in Olympic history."

THE SCANDAL

After three hours and 13 minutes, the Olympic stadium erupted with applause as one runner, New Yorker Fred Lorz, strode into the arena well clear of the pack. A bricklayer by day, who ran through the streets to train at night, Lorz crossed the finish line and was congratulated by Alice Roosevelt, the 20-year-old eldest daughter of President Theodore Roosevelt, who placed a laurel wreath on his head. But there was suddenly a commotion, with a spectator coming forward and declaring Lorz a cheat. He claimed the runner had not completed the entire course. Lorz did not even try to deny the allegations, claiming the entire affair was a joke gone wrong. He said he was at a point of exhaustion after around nine miles, accepting a ride in a car driven by his manager. But the car broke down 10 miles later and Lorz resumed the race, easily beating the field home after his little 'boost'.

Lorz was immediately stripped of the medal, which went to second place-getter Thomas Hicks. A distressed Hicks crossed the line 15 minutes after Lorz, with onlookers helping him in the last few strides, as he was a state of near collapse. His time of 3 hours, 28 minutes and 53 seconds remains the worst in Olympic history.

THE AFTERMATH

It was later revealed that Hicks' minders, seeing him struggling midway through the race, gave him a combination of strychnine and egg whites to keep him on track. When he faltered again, further into the race, they gave him a second dose. Medical experts believe that a third dose may well have killed Hicks. Strychnine, a stimulant, has since been banned, so Hicks may well be able to lay claim to being the first Olympian known to take performance-enhancing drugs. Hicks retired within 24 hours of the race, never competing in big-time athletics again.

Special mention must also go to fourth place-getter, Felix Carvajal from Cuba, who hitchhiked over 700 miles just to get to St Louis to compete. A postman, Carvajal ran the distance in his street clothes. En route, he stopped in an apple orchard, ate some rotten fruit, became physically sick, rested and then resumed . . . and after all that, only just missed out on a medal.

Lorz was banned for life by the Amateur Athletic Union, but reinstated within the year after making a heartfelt apology to all concerned. In 1905, he won the prestigious Boston marathon, legally. He died of pneumonia just nine years later in 1914.

As a result of the scandal of 1904, officials considered striking the marathon from the Olympic program. Fortunately, they decided against the move and the marathon has developed into one of the great sporting spectacles of the modern Olympics.

SKATEGATE ASSAULT, 1994

THE BACKGROUND

Tonya Harding was born to skate. Driven and graceful, she was a child prodigy, landing one of the sport's most difficult moves, the triple lutz, at the age of 12. She left school in her sophomore year to concentrate on her figure skating career. In 1986, when she was just 16, she came sixth in the US Championships and by 1989 was ranked third in the nation. In 1991, she won the US Championships, scoring the event's first-ever 6.0 score for technical merit in the process. The same year, she came second in the world championships. At 1991's Skate America titles, she became the first woman to complete a triple axel in the short program and the first to complete a triple axel with a double toe loop.

Injuries and poor form, however, saw her unable to maintain that standard of excellence and by 1992 she'd dropped to third in the US and finished fourth at the Winter Olympics. She also developed a reputation with some as a 'drama queen' following a series of controversies; she arrived late for the 1992 Winter Olympics, with jetlag cited as a reason for her poor display, and more than once asked referees to re-start her program because of wardrobe and equipment malfunctions. She changed coaches several times.

THE SCANDAL

The night before the 1994 US Figure Skating Championships in Detroit, another star skater, Nancy Kerrigan, completed a practice session. She stopped to speak to a reporter when a man wielding a large baton attacked her, hitting her on the right knee, before fleeing through an exit door. Kerrigan's father carried her to her dressing room before rushing her to hospital, where X-rays showed no break, but severe bruising and swelling. The injuries forced Kerrigan out of the championships and, in her absence, Harding and Michelle Kwan filled the first two slots, winning places in the US Olympic team as a result. But officials decided, because of the bizarre circumstances behind the injury, Kerrigan would be added to the team for the Lillehammer Olympics, with Kwan relegated to an alternate.

The sport was rocked by the Kerrigan attack. Harding claimed she herself had been the victim of death threats, telling a reporter, "It scares me because it could have been anyone here."

Within a week of the attack, police made a breakthrough. Shane Stant, a bounty hunter, turned himself in to police, alleging he had hit Kerrigan at the request of Harding and her former husband, Jeff Gillooly.

By now both Harding and Kerrigan were in Lillehammer and officials considered kicking Harding off the team. But with no hard evidence, she was allowed to stay. The pair lived and trained in close quarters amid a tense atmosphere that captured the world press's imagination. Harding, under enormous pressure, bombed out of medal contention, finishing in eighth spot. Kerrigan looked certain to win gold before being pipped at the post by Russia's Oksana Balul, and had to be content with a silver medal.

THE AFTERMATH

In February 1994, Gillooly accepted a plea bargain in exchange for testimony against Harding. Four men – Gillooly, Stant, the getaway car driver and Harding's former bodyguard, Shawn Eckhardt – all did prison time after an intense police investigation and court case.

In March of the same year, Harding pleaded guilty to conspiring to hinder the prosecution of the attackers. She was placed on probation for three years, made to do 500 hours of community service and fined $160,000. She was also forced to pull out of the 1994 World Figure Skating Championships. Soon afterwards, the US Figure Skating Association stripped Harding of the 1994 national title and banned her for life, as a skater or coach. The USFSA released a statement saying she had shown a "clear disregard for fairness, good sportsmanship and ethical behaviour".

In the years after the scandal, Harding became a professional boxer (winning three of six bouts) and set a land speed record in a vintage gas coupe. She has continually defended her role in the affair. In 2008 she published an autobiography, *The Tonya Tapes*, in which she alleged that she considered going to the FBI with her knowledge of the plot, but decided against it after threats by Gillooly. This has been emphatically denied by Gillooly.

Nancy Kerrigan was inducted into the United States Figure Skating Hall of Fame in 2004 and remains one of the sport's most beloved figures.

TYSON GOES FERAL, 1997

THE BACKGROUND

Mike Tyson hit the pro boxing scene like a tornado, winning his first 19 bouts, all by knockout. He became the youngest world heavyweight champion in history, beating Trevor Berbick to take the WBC crown in 1986 when he was just 20 years and four months old. Within 12 months, he added the WBA and IBF titles to his collection, beating James Smith and Tony Tucker respectively. In doing so, he became the first man to hold all three titles simultaneously. He successfully defended his title nine times, beating fighters like Larry Holmes and Frank Bruno along the way.

But Tyson had a dark side. More than once, he found himself in strife with the law, and in 1992 was convicted of raping an 18-year-old former Miss Rhode Island, Desiree Washington, in Indianapolis. He was sentenced to six years in jail, but released after three. He then went on the comeback trail, scoring easy wins over Peter McNeeley and Buster Mathis Jr, before regaining his WBC crown with a knockout of Frank Bruno 12 months after his release.

THE SCANDAL

In November 1996, Evander Holyfield, a rank outsider, beat Tyson in Las Vegas in a WBA title fight. Tyson's camp complained bitterly afterwards, claiming Holyfield had head-butted their man several times during the bout. The referee ruled the head-butts to be accidental and the pair squared off for a rematch in June 1997, again in Vegas. The bout grossed a record $100 million, Tyson earning $30 million and Holyfield $35 million.

Early in the third round, referee Mills Lane stopped the fight after Tyson bit Holyfield on the ear. Lane warned Tyson, deducting two points from his score as the crowd booed the fighter. "He acted like a man who had just been attacked by a swarm of hornets," Lane said of Holyfield later. "That's when I saw blood streaming from his ear. I didn't want to believe it [that he had been bitten]."

Even though Tyson should have been disqualified, the fight resumed. Tyson bit Holyfield's ear again. This time, Lane disqualified Tyson, awarding the fight to Holyfield. There were wild scenes when Lane announced the fight was over after just three rounds, with fighting breaking out in sections of the crowd and extra police being called in to stop a near-riot. Several spectators in the massive crowd at the MGM Grand Garden Arena had to be treated by paramedics for injuries.

THE AFTERMATH

Holyfield could barely believe the events of that infamous night. "At first when the pain came and I saw him spit the ear out of his mouth, it was a shocking thing," he said later. "Shocking things are supposed to happen to other people. But when I came back straight at him, it was his turn to be shocked. I broke Tyson's heart that night."

Tyson held a press conference and defended his actions, declaring he only bit Holyfield because he had been constantly head-butted again throughout the bout. "Evander, I am sorry," Tyson said. "I will learn from this horrible mistake."

The Nevada State Athletic Commission fined Tyson $3 million, 10 percent of his purse and the maximum fine they were allowed to impose. He was also suspended for life, but permitted to apply for reinstatement of his licence after a year.

In 1999, Tyson was convicted of assaulting two motorists in a road rage incident, serving nine months in jail. He continued to fight and had a shot at regaining a world title against Lennox Lewis in 2002. The pair were due to fight in Las Vegas, but a brawl between the two fighters (and their entourages) resulted in a change of venue to Memphis, Tennessee. Lewis was always in charge and knocked Tyson out in the eighth round. Tyson, who earlier had told Lewis, "I want to eat your children", was gracious in defeat, and the fight set a new record in pay-per-view history of over $106 million.

Tyson had his last professional win against Clifford Etienne early in 2003 and filed for bankruptcy soon afterwards. He quit boxing after a series of poor performances in 2005, never having regained any of his world titles. Despite his controversial career, the influential *Ring* magazine named Tyson 16th when it rated the best 100 boxers of all time in 2003.

AYRTON SENNA'S TRAGIC DEATH, 1994

THE BACKGROUND

Ayrton Senna was a true legend of motor racing. Born into a wealthy Brazilian family in 1960, he had a successful career in karting before making the move to Formula Three and then Formula One. A brilliant driver in difficult conditions, and no stranger to controversy, he held the record for most pole positions until being overtaken in 2006. He remains the third most successful driver of all time in terms of race wins and won the highly rated Monaco Grant Prix a record six times.

Ayrton Senna in 1989.

In 1994, Senna was driving for the Williams team. He had doubts about the new FW16 car, saying before the start of that season, "I have a very negative feeling about driving the car and driving it on the limit ... Some of that is down to the lack of electronic change. Also, the car has its own characteristics, which I'm not fully confident in yet. It's going to be a season with lots of accidents, and I'll risk saying that we'll be lucky if something really serious doesn't happen."

Senna had his poorest start to a Formula One season after making those comments, taking pole position in both the Brazilian and Pacific Grands Prix before failing to finish either one. On the Friday of the San Marino Grand Prix, Senna's close friend Rubens Barrichello was taken to hospital after a bad crash. The following day, driver Roland Ratzenberger died when his Simtek car lost control and crashed at 314kph. Doctor Sid Watkins, who told Senna of Ratzenberger's death, suggested to Senna that he should withdraw from the event and go fishing. Senna declined, but broke down in tears to his girlfriend that night, worrying about the event. On the Sunday morning, he met with fellow driver Alain Prost and the pair resolved to work to improve Formula One safety standards in coming months.

THE SCANDAL

An early crash in the race saw the safety car deployed, but by the sixth lap, the debris had been removed and the race resumed. On the seventh lap, the second held at racing speed, Senna's car left the track at the 190mph Tamburello corner, striking a concrete barrier at great speed. Investigations later showed the car left the track at 310kph and in the two seconds before it hit the barrier, it had slowed to 218kph. The collision tore the right front wheel and nose cone off Senna's car, which spun before finally coming to a halt. It is believed the wheel flew up into the cockpit, striking Senna in the head. The resulting head trauma proved fatal, despite the fact Senna was wearing a helmet. Fire marshalls went to work but it wasn't until medical personnel arrived that Senna was removed from the crumpled vehicle. Doctors performed a tracheotomy on Senna in an attempt to open an airway and allow him to breathe. The Brazilian ace had also lost a lot of blood.

A medical helicopter was called and Senna was rushed to a nearby hospital. But 10 minutes after arrival, doctors confirmed his heart had stopped beating and he was placed on life support. Within three hours, he was pronounced dead.

Italian authorities decided to lay charges against Williams-Renault team principal Frank Williams, team designer Adrian Newey, technical chief Patrick Head, and three others. They were put on trial for manslaughter in 1997, with the prosecution alleging they were responsible for a faulty steering-column weld on Senna's vehicle.

THE AFTERMATH

The sport's ruling body, FIA, threatened to boycott future events in Italy if any of the three were found guilty. All three were acquitted, with that verdict upheld after an appeal two years later. Patrick Head was put on trial a third time and an Italian court decided he was responsible for Senna's death, with the verdict stating, "It has been determined that the accident was caused by a steering column failure. This failure was caused by badly designed and badly executed modifications. The responsibility of this falls on Patrick Head, culpable of omitted control."

Head was not arrested, as the statute of limitations for manslaughter in Italy is seven years and the verdict came 13 years after the accident. Designer Adrian Newey revealed recently that both he and Head had considered walking away from the sport after being traumatised by Senna's death.

Senna's death is regarded by experts as a turning point in motor racing history, with a series of new safety measures introduced after his tragic crash and the re-introduction of the Grand Prix Drivers' Association. He was the last man to die in a Formula One race.

MEDIA MOGUL HIJACKS AUSTRALIAN CRICKET, 1977

THE BACKGROUND

World cricket was in a volatile state in the mid 1970s. Despite the sport's massive surge in popularity, players were convinced they were not being paid what they were worth and cried out for change. Enter Australian media baron Kerry Packer, owner of the Nine Television Network. Packer approached the Australian Cricket Board with a lucrative offer to televise the game and thereby raise revenue. Packer threw a massive $1.5 million over three years at the Board, around eight times what the national broadcaster, the ABC, was paying at the time. But the Board felt a loyalty to the government-owned ABC, the game's traditional broadcaster, and rejected Packer's offer.

Undeterred, Packer tried a different plan. With the assistance of businessmen John Cornell and Austin Robertson, he created a plan for a series of Tests and one-day internationals between Australia and the rest of the world. But again, the Australian Cricket Board was not interested.

THE SCANDAL

Furious at the rebuff, Packer set about secretly signing the world's best cricketers to contracts to play in his own breakaway competition, World Series Cricket, early in 1977. Former Australian captain Ian Chappell helped sign many of the Test team to Packer's cause, offering contracts far greater than the players, then mostly part-timers, were on at the time. England captain Tony Greig came on board with the scheme, adding many of the best British players to the rebels.

Australia toured England in May 1977, with 13 of the 17 Aussie players signed to Packer. But news of the breakaway leaked out during the tour and there was an immediate backlash.

The Australian players were threatened with being sacked from the Test team, while Greig was stripped of the England captaincy. A handful of players, most notably Australian fast bowler Jeff Thomson, pulled out of the breakaway, but most players remained steadfast. Friendships were destroyed, with many of the rebels branded 'traitors' for abandoning the establishment.

The International Cricket Council entered the drama, meeting with Packer. But the parties could not find common ground and the matter went to court in England. Packer won the case, with the judge ruling players were entitled to make a living and the ICC should not stand in their way. But legal restrictions were designed to make it hard for what was dubbed 'the Packer circus'. The Australian team could not call themselves 'Australia' (they became WSC Australian XI), play at cricket's traditional venues, use the game's official rules, which were owned by the ICC, or play official 'Test matches'.

Despite the setbacks, Packer ploughed ahead, and the first 'Supertest' was played at Melbourne's VFL Park in December 1977 between WSC Australian XI and a West Indian team.

THE AFTERMATH

World Series Cricket had a tentative start with an unsure public, but grew in popularity, with the new one-day games a huge hit. Packer played many of his games under lights, with players wearing coloured clothing, unheard of in cricket before that, and steadily gained crowds and television ratings. There were other innovations – coloured balls and pitches that were grown in greenhouses before being dropped into the middle of fields, and effects microphones and cameras in the stumps, giving fans a new view of the action. Channel Nine also used a camera behind the bowler at both ends of the field, rather than showing all the action from one end, and the viewers loved it. It brought the game a newfound link with commercialism, the World Series jingle 'C'mon Aussie C'mon' becoming an iconic catch-cry for Australia at the time.

All the players were by now banned from traditional cricket and a virtual second-string Australian side was thrashed 5-1 by England in the home Test series in 1978–79. But both sides were feeling the pinch of fighting a costly war for a relatively small audience and after two years, a compromise was reached. ACB Board Chairman Bob Parish announced a truce in May 1979, with the kicker being that Packer's Nine Network would not only televise the game, but also handle cricket's marketing through a newly formed corporation, PBL Marketing.

Packer died in 2005, but his Nine Network has continued to telecast the game ever since. There remains some ill-feeling about the revolution that changed the game in the late 1970s, with the ICC refusing to include the results or players' performances from the two seasons of World Series Cricket in their official records.

DIVER'S HIV REVELATION, 1994

THE BACKGROUND

Greg Louganis is the best-known athlete in the history of diving. Like Tiger Woods in golf and Michael Jordan in basketball, he was an individual who rewrote the record books and brought his sport a new, higher profile, by attracting vast new audiences and acclaim throughout the world, and came to define his sport.

Born in California in 1960, of Samoan and Swedish descent, he was put up for adoption when he was less than a year old and raised by a couple who encouraged him to do gymnastics and dancing to overcome asthma. From there, he graduated to trampolining and soon made the progression to diving.

Former Olympic champion Sammy Lee took Louganis under his wing and, at just 16, the youngster competed at the 1976 Olympics. He won silver in the 10 metre

Gold-medal winning diver Greg Louganis, years later in 2009.

platform and two years later won the world title. He missed the 1980 Olympics due to the US boycott, but two years later, at the World Championships, became the first diver to score a perfect 10 from all seven judges.

At the 1984 Olympics, he won the 10 metre platform and three metre springboard double, and repeated the feat at the 1988 Olympics. He received worldwide acclaim for his performance in Seoul, after crashing into the springboard with his head during a mistimed jump in the preliminary rounds. "I jumped off the board and heard this big clank," Louganis said later. "That's my perception of the dive."

Despite suffering a cut head that required stitching and being badly shaken by the incident, Louganis won the gold medal by a commanding 25-point margin.

THE SCANDAL

In 1994, Louganis announced he was gay, attending the Gay Games as an announcer and putting on a special diving exhibition that drew massive crowds. The following year, he released a tell-all autobiography, *Breaking the Silence*. Louganis revealed how his early life was marred by domestic abuse and rape, and how that resulted in him suffering from depression. He also declared he was HIV-positive. Louganis learned he had the AIDS virus six months before the Seoul Olympics, when that fateful dive saw his infected blood trickle into the pool. Louganis' doctor had put him on the anti-retroviral drug AZT, which he took every four hours around the clock in a bid to slow the deadly virus and keep him in shape for the Olympics Games.

Upon this revelation, officials and some fellow divers questioned whether the champion should have announced he was HIV-positive when his blood entered the pool, fearing fellow divers could become infected. Louganis himself had a crisis of conscience about whether to reveal his condition, particularly when he was stitched up by the US team doctor, James Puffer, who did not wear gloves at the time. "Do I say something?" Louganis pondered years later. "You know, this has been an incredibly guarded secret."

The fears were later proven to be unfounded by medical experts at the US Centers for Disease Control and Prevention, however, with thousands of gallons of water and strong chlorine ensuring there would have been no risk of transmitting the virus.

THE AFTERMATH

Louganis revealed his inner torment leading into the Seoul Olympics, years later. "Dealing with HIV was really difficult for me because I felt like, God, the US Olympic Committee needs to know this," he said. "US Diving needs to know it because what if I get sick at the Olympic Games and am unable to compete?"

Many of Louganis' sponsors dropped him when he revealed his condition, the exception being swimsuit maker Speedo. Louganis' confession, followed by basketball superstar Magic Johnson's revelation that he had AIDS in 1991, changed the way sports stars were treated by doctors and in some cases, changed the rules of their games. Doctors and trainers began wearing latex gloves when treating players, while those who are bleeding are now required to leave the field until the wound is treated in most sports.

The panic expressed by some fellow competitors and critics when the AIDS outbreak was at its height has now lessened. Medical experts believe there is virtually no chance of contracting the virus from a fellow competitor on the playing field, and only one athlete, a social soccer player in Italy, is suspected to have become infected after having clashed heads with a player who was HIV-positive. The IOC considered testing athletes for HIV, but rejected the idea.

Nowdays, Greg Louganis travels the world with athletes like Peggy Fleming, Bruce Jenner and Jackie Joyner-Kersee, to tell of their lives in sport while living with a chronic disease.

"It's just telling my story really," he says. "I want to be remembered as a strong and graceful diver, but as a person, I want to be remembered as someone who made a difference."

THE UNDERARM BOWLING SAGA, 1981

THE BACKGROUND

Australia and New Zealand have always been fierce rivals on the sporting field, but never more so than in cricket's Benson and Hedges World Series in 1981. Going into the final game before a massive crowd at the Melbourne Cricket Ground, the series was tied at one-all. Australia won the first match and New Zealand hit back with an upset win in the second. But the game had another major controversy, long before the infamous final ball, involving Australian captain Greg Chappell.

Midway through the Australian innings, Chappell was batting when he hit a high ball into the outfield. Kiwi fielder Martin Snedden dived and took what appeared to be a spectacular catch close to the ground. The umpires were unsure if the catch was 'clean'; video replays could not be used by the officials in that era and Chappell refused to walk. The catch was denied. The Kiwis were clearly miffed and much, much worse was to come. Chappell went on to score 90 as Australia compiled a respectable 235-4 in 50 overs.

With opening batsman Bruce Edgar scoring a century, the Kiwis slowly chipped away at the Aussie total. Entering the 50th and final over, they needed 15 runs to win. They belted two boundaries, but also lost two wickets, Ian Smith and Richard Hadlee. That brought tail-end batsman Brian McKechnie to the crease, needing six runs off the final delivery and tie the match.

THE SCANDAL

Chappell approached the bowler, his younger brother Trevor, and instructed him to bowl the last delivery along the ground underarm, effectively making it impossible for McKechnie to hit the ball over the fence for a six. Although within the rules, the tactic is unheard of in the modern game and regarded as unfair, or 'not cricket'. Greg Chappell informed the umpires of his plan and they conferred, unsure of what to do. But as the rules permitted underarm bowling, they reluctantly agreed to allow Chappell to go ahead.

Australian wicket-keeper Rodney Marsh could be heard muttering his disapproval of the decision, moments before Trevor Chappell delivered the ball. As confusion reigned, one Aussie fielder, legendary paceman Dennis Lillee, wandered outside the fielding circles on the field. That meant that the delivery was technically a no-ball, and should have been bowled again, but the umpires failed to detect Lillee's error. Trevor Chappell bowled the ball underarm to a stunned McKechnie.

"The umpires told me it was going to be underarm and I had no idea what to do, to be honest," McKechnie said two decades later. "It was almost 100 metres to the boundary. I decided I wasn't going to have a swing and get bowled."

In the end, McKechnie merely blocked the ball, and the game was over with Australia winning by six runs. But as sections of the crowd, even many Australian fans, booed the home team, McKechnie tossed his bat away in anger. Edgar, the non-striking batsman at the other end, made a rude gesture with his fingers at Trevor Chappell. "Throwing the bat was just frustration," McKechnie recalled. "It was a hell of a good game of cricket. I'm sure Greg wishes he had never given the instruction and Trevor wishes he never had to carry it out. Everyone has times in their life when you look back and think, 'Geez, I wish I hadn't done that.'"

THE AFTERMATH

As the ball was being bowled, Ian Chappell, the eldest of the three brothers, was commentating on the game on Australian national television. "No, Greg, no, you can't do that," Ian Chappell declared, echoing the thoughts of two nations.

New Zealand Prime Minister Robert Muldoon slammed the actions of the Chappells, labelling it "the most disgusting incident I can recall in the history of cricket". In a tirade in Parliament, he added, "It was an act of pure cowardice and I consider it appropriate that the Australian team was wearing yellow." The Australians also earned a rebuke from their own Prime Minister, Malcolm Fraser, who described the incident as "contrary to the traditions of the game". Ironically, it was McKechnie who found himself in hot water with cricket officials, censured for "bringing the game into disrepute" when he angrily threw his bat away.

Years later, Greg Chappell described the incident as a cry for help when he was mentally and physically drained from his role as national captain. Chappell was in the midst of a series of disputes between officials and players at the time, causing him considerable stress. "I wasn't fit, I mean, I was mentally wrung out," Chappell explained in an interview with the ABC. "I was fed up with the whole system, things that seemed to be just closing in on us, and I suppose in my own case I felt they were closing in on me, and it was a cry for help."

Soon after the incident, the International Cricket Council banned underarm bowling, saying it was "not in the spirit of the game".

WOMEN'S GOLF BALL-MOVING ACCUSATION, 1972

THE BACKGROUND

In the 1970s, New Hampshire-born Jane Blalock was one of women's golf's most talented players. Born in Portsmouth in 1945, she went to college in Florida and won the New Hampshire Amateur title for five straight years in the 1960s while working as a schoolteacher. That earned her a place in New Hampshire's Top 10 Athletes of the Century and she also went on to become a New England Sports Hall of Fame member.

After impressive efforts as an amateur, she decided to turn professional in 1969 and was voted LPGA Tour Rookie of the Year, after an impressive maiden season. From her rookie year until her last event in 1980, Blalock never missed a cut on tour, a record for 299 tournaments that still stands today. She won her first pro tournament, the Lady Carling Open, in Marietta, Georgia, in 1970. She won two tournaments in 1971, the George Washington Classic and the Lady Pepsi Open, before taking out the prestige Dinah Shore Colgate Winner's Circle in California in 1972. Ironically, Blalock would never win a major in her career, although years after taking this event, it was elevated to LPGA major status.

Blalock quickly developed a reputation as a tough competitor. A month after winning the Dinah Shore event, she took out the Suzuki Golf Internationale, before her world came crashing down.

THE SCANDAL

Playing in the Bluegrass Invitational in Louisiville, Kentucky in 1972, Blalock was disqualified for allegedly signing an incorrect scorecard at the end of the second round. The tournament director, Gene McAuliff, announced that Blalock had been barred from the event for not marking her ball, per regulations, on the 17th green. She had also failed to take a two-stroke penalty for that infraction, as stated in the rules, and was fined $500.

A few days later, the LPGA board went a step further, suspending Blalock for a year for "actions inconsistent with the code of ethics of the organisation". After an internal investigation, the board said that Blalock had been under scrutiny for more than a year and had allegedly been caught moving her ball illegally on several occasions. The LPGA claimed that Blalock broke down in tears and admitted her guilt when confronted with the evidence – Blalock denied any such admission and began legal action.

Blalock was the tour's leading money-earner for the year at the time of her suspension in June 1972, but was soon snubbed by her fellow players. "The last few weeks I'd walk into a roomful of people talking and they'd stop when they saw me," she said at the time. "It was like everyone knew something except me. It was a feeling of complete anxiety. I couldn't eat. I'd lie in bed with my eyes open. If I ever came close to losing my mind, it was then. They were playing games with a person's life. I don't think they realise it."

THE AFTERMATH

Blalock took her fight to the courts, winning an early battle in June 1972, when a judge allowed her to keep playing on the LPGA tour while her case was being heard, with any money she won in that time being placed in a special trust fund. She sued the LPGA for $5 million. Several players testified that they saw Blalock move her ball, while others argued her $500 fine, disqualification and probation in Louisville was not a strong enough penalty. Her former coach Bob Toski said, "She has a compulsion to win. I think she needs psychiatric help." At least one player, Sandra Palmer, defended Blalock, saying she had never seen her break the rules. An LPGA official claimed he had suggested to Blalock that she should feign injury to avoid adverse publicity from the case, but that the star refused.

In August 1974, Blalock finally won her case against the LPGA and was awarded $4,500 in damages. Blalock amended her damages suit from the original $5 million to $4,500, the amount she says she could have won in the 1972 Lady Carling tournament, the one event from which she was banned. A year later, the damages were tripled, and the LPGA had to pay Blalock's court costs, which came to nearly $100,000.

Blalock overcame the drama, continuing to star on the LPGA tour. She was the first woman to win $100,000 in prize money for four straight years, and has the most wins of any golfer not inducted into the LPGA Hall of Fame.

ITALIAN SOCCER BETTING-GATE, 2011

THE BACKGROUND

There have long been suspicions about players throwing games and organised crime involvement in Italian soccer. In 2006, the world famous Juventus club was relegated for a season and other clubs reprimanded. But Italy went on to win the World Cup the same year and Italians hoped they had heard the last of corruption in their beloved game. But in 2011, when a group of players including superstar Giuseppe Signori were arrested on match-fixing charges, the entire nation was in shock. Few could have realised that this was just the tip of the iceberg, with more revelations to come.

When the first arrests were made, it barely made news outside Italy, as the scandal mainly involved lower division clubs (known as Series B and C in Italy) and, apart from Signori, few big names. Another exception was Atalanta captain Cristiano Doni, who in August 2011 was banned for three and a half years, effectively ending his career. His Atalanta club was docked six points for the 2011–12 season. The Ascoli Calcio club was also deducted six points, while other clubs were fined and in some cases relegated to lower divisions. A wide-ranging crackdown resulted in 20 players being banned for periods of one to five years, and Italian soccer claimed it had rid itself of the stain of corruption.

THE SCANDAL

In December 2011, Italian police began phase two of their investigations, arresting a string of players and officials. Doni, already found guilty and banned, was arrested again, this time, it would seem, to prevent him from tampering with evidence. The police prosecutor Roberto di Martino dropped a bomb, declaring he feared the scandal had connections with criminals worldwide. "One of the suspects has admitted that these operations have been going on for 10 years," di Martino said. "At the top of the organisation are men from Singapore, who are those who move the money, but the shareholders are divided from the West, to the Far East, to South America and they manage with their men how to change the outcome of football matches."

That statement resulted in the scandal, now dubbed 'Scommessopoli' (Betting-gate), coming to the attention of the international media. The football world watched in awe as more and more high-profile players and managers were implicated, and many arrested by police. In May 2012, police began another wave of raids. Some players were placed under house arrest and others banned from leaving the country.

Italian national team manager Cesare Prandelli said that he would understand if his team was kicked out of the prestigious Euro 2012 tournament, but this did not happen. In July, another group of clubs was fined and deducted points, with more players receiving lengthy bans.

THE AFTERMATH

Juventus manager Conte was suspended until the end of the 2012–13 season, for not reporting two instances of match-fixing during his time at the helm of Siena. He appealed the decision, and lost, before his suspension was reduced to four months. Juventus issued a statement backing Conte.

Some stood up to the corruption, showing great courage. Gubbio star Simone Farina was one such player, earning praise from FIFA boss Sepp Blatter for blowing the whistle on the corrupt affair; Farina told officials he had been offered €200,000 to fix a Coppa Italia match between Cesena and Gubbio.

Italian premier Mario Monti was so shocked by the extent of the rorting that he said he believed the country should suspend its major competitions for two years in a bid to get clean. Further investigations revealed the match-fixing scandal was not restricted to Italian games, and the full extent of the corruption may never be known. The affair is ongoing, with police and prosecutors continuing their inquiries as Italian soccer fans brace themselves for the next scandal to unfold. Police, meanwhile, are attempting to institute a ban on betting on the outcome of matches in Italy, believing it to be the only surefire way of putting an end to the cycle of corruption.

MCLAREN EMPLOYEES SPY ON FERRARI, 2007

THE BACKGROUND

Ferrari were seen to be at the cutting edge of F1 motor racing in the late 1990s. But one of Ferrari's key executives, engineer Nigel Stepney, was unhappy with the team's restructuring after the departure of technical director Ross Brawn and talked of leaving for a rival F1 team. "I really want to move forward with my career and that's something that's not happening right now," he complained early in 2007. "I'd like to move into a new environment here at Ferrari but if an opportunity arose with another team I would definitely consider it."

The Ferrari factory and office, 2006.

Not wanting to lose the highly regarded Stepney, who turned the company around in the 1990s, Ferrari put him in charge of Team Performance Development. The role was more behind-the-scenes and would result in Stepney attending fewer actual races.

Tension between rival race teams ran high that season. At the Monaco Grand Prix in May, a white powder was detected in the fuel tank of Felipe Massa's car. A sample of the powder was taken and sent to police. There were allegations the powder was an attempted act of sabotage by Stepney. Several fingers were pointed, but he insisted he was the victim of a dirty tricks campaign by police and rival teams.

THE SCANDAL

In June 2007, Ferrari filed a complaint against Stepney, resulting in a criminal investigation by the district attorney of Modena in Italy. Police also staged a surprise raid on Stepney's home near Ferrari's base at Maranello in northern Italy. Three weeks later, a sports magazine reported that Ferrari had sacked Stepney, allegedly based on the findings of its own internal investigation. A Ferrari spokesman told a TV news show that Stepney's dismissal arose after "irregularities discovered at the Ferrari factory prior to the Monaco Grand Prix".

Ferrari also announced it had taken action against a McLaren engineer, later named as Mike Coughlan. McLaren subsequently suspended Coughlan while police issued a search warrant of his home. It was alleged that Coughlan had been in possession of over 700 pages of Ferrari paperwork, photocopied in a shop. Ferrari had no idea of the industrial sabotage until they were tipped off by an employee at the photocopying shop. Late in 2007, Ferrari dropped a High Court case against Coughlan and his wife in exchange for full disclosure of their knowledge of the scandal and the promise of future cooperation. McLaren declared the results of its own investigation, which they said showed "no Ferrari materials or data are or have ever been in the possession of any McLaren employee other than the individual sued by Ferrari".

Also in 2007, Renault's F1 team was called before the FIA World Motorsport Council, charged with obtaining secret information about McLaren's 2006–07 models. It was alleged that Renault F1 had intimate details of McLaren's engine, suspension and fueling system. The charges were alleged to revolve around a McLaren employee who had switched teams to Renault.

THE AFTERMATH

McLaren declared its investigation showed "no Ferrari intellectual property has been passed to any other members of the team or incorporated into [our] cars". McLaren invited the FIA to inspect its cars to confirm this. A week later, McLaren was summoned by the FIA to a meeting of the World Motor Council. At the meeting, the FIA found that Vodafone McLaren Mercedes was in breach of article 151C of the International Sporting Code. But the FIA had no evidence that McLaren actually used the information and did not hand down any penalty, reserving the right to do so. Angry Ferrari officials described the decision as "incomprehensible".

The FIA re-opened the case in September 2007, finding McLaren guilty of obtaining information from Ferrari to confer a dishonest and fraudulent sporting advantage. McLaren lost all its points, was excluded from competing in the 2007 Constructors' Championship, was fined a record $100 million and ordered to submit its 2008 engine design for scrutiny. McLaren drivers Fernando Alonso and Lewis Hamilton did not lose their points, however, and were allowed to continue competing because of their cooperation. Renault was also found guilty of breaching the International Sporting Code, but was not penalised.

McLaren put out a press release, admitting "a number of McLaren employees" accessed Ferrari information, and apologised for the affair. In 2010, Stepney was sentenced to a year and eight months in prison by an Italian court and fined £500.

YUGOSLAV BASKETBALL'S CIVIL WAR, 1990

THE BACKGROUND

Vlade Divac and Dražen Petrović were superbly talented Yugoslav basketball players, who went on to showcase their skills in the NBA. They were among a number of pioneers who opened the floodgates for players from Europe to make the leap into the game's best competition, but long before that they were stars of the Yugoslav team that was the pride of Europe. Divac was a Serb and Petrović a Croatian, but above that, they were both Yugoslavians, and members of a team that proved among the most exciting in world basketball in the 1980s and early 1990s. The pair were instrumental in Yugoslavia winning the bronze medal at the 1986 FIBA World Championships and silver behind the Soviet Union at the 1988 Seoul Olympics. Petrović, a brilliant individual, was the game's top scorer with 24 points, as the Russians ground out a 76-63 win. That performance gave the Yugoslavs confidence and two years later, in 1990, they wrote their names into their country's folklore by taking the gold medal in the FIBA World Championships. This time they turned the tables on the Russians, winning 92-75 in Argentina.

The pair were, by that point, NBA stars – Divac with the LA Lakers and Petrović with the Portland Trail Blazers – and played key roles in Yugoslavia's upset victory. They were best friends and national heroes, but what at first seemed a trivial incident, moments after the final ended, soon changed everything.

THE SCANDAL

The Yugoslavs' win prompted jubilant fans to charge onto the court to greet their heroes. One of the fans was waving a Croatian flag (Croatia is one of six areas that made up Yugoslavia, at a time of great tension between rival ethnic groups). The man approached Divac, who told him he should have been celebrating with a Yugoslav national flag and not a Croatian one. The man allegedly made an abusive remark about the Yugoslav flag in response, at which point Divac grabbed the Croatian flag from him and crumpled it up. With Yugoslavia already on the brink of civil war, political activists seized on the incident. Divac became the hero of the Serbians and was an instant villain among the Croats.

Civil war broke out in Yugoslavia in 1991, becoming a bloody battle that shocked the world and saw atrocities committed on both sides. The turmoil only added to the tension between Divac and several of his former national team-mates, who were Croats. The war dragged on to 1995, when Croatia formed its own breakaway team for the EuroBasket tournament. Yugoslavia took out the event, with Croatia coming in third. But at the medal ceremony, the Croats received their bronze medals and then stormed off the podium before the Yugoslavs were presented with their golds.

THE AFTERMATH

Vlade Divac went on to become one of the most successful and popular European imports ever to play in the NBA. He is one of only six players in NBA history to score 13,000 points, make 9,000 rebounds, produce 3,000 assists and 1,500 blocked shots. He was the first player born and trained outside the US to play 1,000 NBA games and played 16 seasons in the NBA, earning over $93 million. But he was forever haunted by the incident at the 1990 World Championships and said years later he regretted the spur of the moment reaction to the Croatian flag. He had no idea at the time the trouble it would cause, above all ending his close friendship with Petrović. Sadly, the pair never reconciled.

While Divac had blossomed in the NBA, Dražen Petrović struggled at the Trail Blazers. He was unable to get a starting position with the team and had thoughts of going home, but helped overcome his homesickness by regular talks with Divac when the pair were still friends. A move to the New Jersey Nets saw him become one of the best shooting guards in the NBA, but in 1993, Petrović died in Germany, when a car driven by his girlfriend smashed into a truck. He was just 28 years old.

After his death, the great Michael Jordan said, "It was a thrill to play against Dražen. Every time we competed, he competed with an aggressive attitude. So, we've had some great battles in the past and unfortunately, they were short battles." Over 100,000 people attended his funeral, while the city of Zagreb named a town square in his honour.

The civil wars in Yugoslavia throughout the 1990s cost an estimated 140,000 lives.

BUDD AND DECKER COLLIDE, 1984

THE BACKGROUND

An outstanding long-distance runner, Zola Budd achieved great success in a short career on the international stage. But her career was dogged by controversy, which may have prevented the quietly spoken runner from producing her best.

Born in Bloemfontein in 1966, Budd was just 17 when she shattered the world 5,000 metres world record. What's more, she did it running barefoot. Budd preferred to run without shoes and did so from her early childhood. Because her record time of 15:01:83 was run in South Africa, however, which was barred from international sports due to its apartheid policy, the International Amateur Athletics Federation refused to ratify it.

Budd's grandfather was British and the same year she broke the world record, in 1984, Budd decided to make a bid to join the British Olympic team. With South Africa barred from competing, Budd was thrown a lifeline by Britain and her application for citizenship was fast-tracked to allow her to compete. Several media organisations and high-profile politicians helped speed up the process to allow Budd to become a British citizen in time for the Olympics. But the move created a storm, with opponents of apartheid furious with the preferential treatment Budd received, and she was the subject of heated debate.

Soon after arriving in England, she was forced to pull out of a race in Sussex when local officials, feeling the pressure and worried about possible protests, withdrew her invitation at the last minute. But that was nothing compared with the drama Budd would create when she competed at the Los Angeles Olympics later that year.

THE SCANDAL

Budd arrived in Los Angeles and the media built up the 3,000 metres race as a battle between her and American world champion Mary Decker. The pair led the way early on, with Romanian Maricica Puica, who had run the fastest time that year to date, also in contention.

After 1,700 metres, Decker and Budd had a minor collision, the impact throwing Budd off balance. She managed to regain her stride after a few paces, but a few seconds later they clashed again, this time more heavily. Budd's left foot struck Decker's thigh, again causing Budd to stumble. She was slightly ahead of Decker, but staggered into the path of the American. Decker's spiked shoe came down on Budd's bare ankle, drawing blood.

Budd can be seen in video footage to wince from the pain of the impact. But Decker had greater problems from the collision, losing balance and stumbling. In a desperate attempt to regain her balance, she grabbed at Budd, ripping the number off the back of the South African's shirt. Decker then totally lost balance, crashing to the ground on the infield as the rest of the field kept running. She injured her hip and was unable to continue. Decker screamed out – a combination of rage and horror that her Olympic dream had ended.

Budd faded in the final stages of the race, with Puica taking the gold medal from Britian's Wendy Smith-Sly and Canada's Lynn Williams. Budd finished a distant seventh to a chorus of boos from angry American fans, who believed she deliberately felled the hometown favourite. Budd was disqualified by a track judge, adding to the crowd's anger.

THE AFTERMATH

A furious Decker told the media that Budd's actions were intentional and cost her a gold medal. Five years later, Budd wrote her autobiography and revealed she deliberately slowed down in the final stages of the race, because she did not want to receive a medal to the boos of hostile fans. Her time of 8 minutes, 37 seconds was more than 10 seconds behind her best, recorded not long before the Olympics began.

Despite being blamed by both Decker and the crowd for the collision, an IAAF jury later ruled she was not at fault over the incident. It is usually considered the trailing athlete's job (in this case Decker) to avoid a collision in such circumstances. Years later, Decker said, "The reason I fell, some people think she tripped me deliberately. I happen to know that wasn't the case at all. The reason I fell is because I am and was very inexperienced in running in a pack."

The pair made their peace years later, but the coldness remains. "She's forgiven me, but she still blames me," Budd has said. Remarkably, Budd has never watched footage of her fateful collision with Decker, which was recently ranked among the 100 greatest sporting moments of all time by a British TV station.

GERMAN SOCCER REF THROWN INTO JAIL, 2005

THE BACKGROUND

Robert Hoyzer came from a proud football-officiating family. His father was a leading referee in West Germany in the 1970s and Hoyzer's aim was to follow in his footsteps. Born in West Berlin in 1979, Hoyzer played junior soccer but always preferred refereeing, and after studying sports management, was registered by the German Football Association as a referee in 2001. He began his professional career in the third division, Regionallia Nord, in the 2001–02 season, handling nine games. The following year, he earned promotion to the second division, controlling 13 games. His reputation began to grow as a fit, young official not afraid of making the hard calls, and before long he was a regular in the second division, known as the 2nd Bundesliga. He never got to the first division where the glamour clubs played, but did control several games in the German Cup, the equivalent of England's FA Cup, a competition that featured many of the best teams in the country.

His biggest job came early in 2005, when he controlled a game between Hamburger SV, a first division club, and minnows Paderborn. Hamburger were hot favourites to win the game and took an early 2-0 lead. But Hoyzer sent off Hamburger striker Emile Mpenza in the first half and awarded Paderborn two dubious penalties, with Paderborn winning 4-2.

THE SCANDAL

Whispers began circulating that Hoyzer had bet on Paderborn to win the game and collected a considerable sum in the wake of their upset victory. Four referees went to the German Football Association with their suspicions about Hoyzer. Hoyzer resigned as the whispers turned into roars and the German Football Association announced it had launched an investigation into the referee. The German prosecutor's office also opened its own inquiry.

After initially denying any wrongdoing, Hoyzer eventually admitted he had ties with organised crime figures, who had been betting large sums on games. He also alleged that other referees and several players were also on the payroll. Hoyzer began to assist police in their investigation and early in February 2005, police raided 19 houses and businesses in a massive sting operation, claiming 25 people were involved. Among them were 14 players and three other referees. Hoyzer also claimed the conspiracy extended beyond Germany, with the gambling ring in regular contact with several senior referees throughout Europe who controlled big games.

Hoyzer, despite his cooperation, was handed a lifetime ban from refereeing football matches throughout Germany. Hoyzer was then arrested by police, who claimed he had fixed several more matches than he had admitted to. In November 2005, Hoyzer was given a jail term of two years and five months. "It wasn't a youthful misdemeanour but a serious crime," judge Gerti Kramer explained. "He violated his important duty of neutrality." Fellow referee Dominik Marks was jailed for one year and six months and also banned for life.

THE AFTERMATH

Hoyzer appealed against the conviction in November 2006, on the grounds that even though he cheated, he had not committed a criminal fraud, but the conviction and charge stood. Police believe the betting ring netted profits of over two million euros before it was detected and dismantled. They believe no first division games were involved, but that some games in the lucrative German Cup were affected. Their investigations found Hoyzer had regular meetings with a crime gang based in Berlin in the lead-up to the scandal. The gang allegedly had close links to several players.

German officials introduced several new measures to stamp out any possibility of further corruption. They changed appointments of referees from four days before games to two days, making it harder for criminals to 'get to' officials. Referees promoted up to the second division were placed under a probation period and a fourth official was given powers to oversee their performances. They brought in a system whereby officials could be suspended at short notice if there were suspicions about their games, while they also monitored sports betting on games more closely. The German Football Association reviewed a series of games it believed were tainted by corrupt officials, replaying them where possible and paying compensation to clubs adversely affected. In 2011, six years after the scandal, Robert Hoyzer was given permission to return to soccer, but as an amateur player in a small local league team.

JIM THORPE STRIPPED OF HIS MEDALS, 1913

THE BACKGROUND

Born in 1888, Jim Thorpe was one of world sport's first true superstars. A native American, he was an extremely versatile athlete who won Olympic gold medals in pentathlon and decathlon, and played professional football, baseball and basketball.

Thorpe was described as a 'natural' sportsman. He excelled at a host of other sports, including the high jump and lacrosse – he even won the 1912 intercollegiate ballroom dancing championship. He starred in both college and pro football, first coming to national attention in 1911 when, playing as a running back, defensive back, placekicker and punter, he scored all his team's points as his college, Carlisle, scored a stunning 18-15 win over top-ranked Harvard. Carlisle, with Thorpe the driving force, went on to claim the national collegiate championship the following year.

Legendary athlete Jim Thorpe.

The same year, he tried out for the Olympic team in high jump, long jump, hurdles, shot put, pole vaulting, javelin, discus and hammer and 56lb weight throwing. He won gold in both the pentathlon and decathlon, despite some setbacks. At one stage of the competition, someone stole his shoes. He found a replacement pair that did not match, in a rubbish bin, and still proved far too good for the field. Thorpe became an instant national hero, receiving a ticker-tape parade through New York on his return from Sweden.

THE SCANDAL

A year after his Olympic success, a newspaper published a story that Thorpe had played professional baseball in North Carolina in 1909–10. The story was, in essence, correct, but Thorpe had received just $2 per game for his efforts. The practice was a common one at the time, with many talented athletes playing pro ball to supplement their incomes, but most did so using aliases and so got away with the ruse.

At the time, the Olympic Games had very strict rules regarding amateurism, completely barring anyone who had ever been paid for playing sport. The Amateur Athletic Union immediately launched an inquiry. Thorpe wrote a letter to the AAU, admitting his mistake. "I hope I will be partly excused by the fact that I was simply an Indian schoolboy and did not know all about such things," he wrote. "In fact, I did not know that I was doing wrong, because I was doing what I knew several other college men had done, except that they did not use their own names."

Admitting his guilt proved to be a mistake – the AAU and International Olympic Commission both revoked Thorpe's amateur status. The IOC went a step further, stripping him of his gold medals, despite Olympic rules, which clearly declared that protests had to be made within a month of the Games concluding (the entire affair did not erupt until the early months of 1913, nearly six months after Thorpe's gold medal wins).

THE AFTERMATH

While Thorpe was devastated to lose his medals, the fact that he was now officially a "professional" resulted in a flood of offers for his services. He played pro baseball for the famed New York Giants in 1913, and went on to play for several other teams in a 10-year career. The same year, he began playing professional football for Indiana team Pine Village before signing a rich deal with the Canton Bulldogs in 1915. He became the first president of the American Professional Football Association, which evolved into the NFL, and continued to play pro football until the age of 41.

Despite making good money in his career, Thorpe struggled financially after retirement during the Great Depression. He got several roles as an extra in Western movies, playing Indian chiefs, and was employed in various other jobs, including as a construction worker, nightclub bouncer and US Merchant Marine. He battled alcoholism throughout his latter years and died of heart failure in 1953, aged 64.

There were several attempts after his death to have his medals returned and his name reinstated in the record books. Finally, in 1982, with the support of the US Congress, the IOC executive committee found in Thorpe's favour. He was given his Olympic title back and two of his children were presented with commemorative medals. In a poll of fans conducted by ABC Sports in 2000, Thorpe was voted the greatest athlete of the twentieth century, beating the likes of Jesse Owens, Muhammad Ali, Babe Ruth, Michael Jordan and Jack Nicklaus.

PHANTOM HORSE WINS IN FOG, 1990

THE BACKGROUND

The Delta Downs track in Vinton, Louisiana was built in a picturesque location. Carved out of a bayou in the extreme south-west corner of the state, it gave punters some charming views of the landscape. But there was a downside to the track's location – when the fog rolled in, it was as thick as pea soup. Long sections of the track would be obscured from the view of the grandstand, and punters had to wait with bated breath as their horses disappeared into the mist, only to re-emerge what seemed an age later.

On one particular day in January 1990, the fog was alarmingly heavy, even by Delta Downs standards. Stewards toyed with the idea of abandoning the meet, but went ahead anyway. In the feature event, the one-mile race, horses would begin in a straightaway, pass the grandstand, circle the entire track once and then finish as they passed the grandstand a second time. And punters were treated to an amazing sight on this day, with a horse called Landing Officer winning the feature event by a stunning 24 lengths. Even more remarkable was the fact that Landing Officer was a 23-1 longshot, with little or no form to rave about. The few punters lucky enough to have backed the unheralded colt sprinted to the betting window to collect, but were stopped in their tracks when the protest light suddenly came on.

THE SCANDAL

Rival jockeys and stewards immediately smelt a rat, and it wasn't just because the unfancied colt had come within 1.2 seconds of shattering the long-standing course record for the mile. Stunned jockeys reported they had not even seen five-year-old Landing Officer in the early stages of the race, thinking it had failed to start or dropped out.

The Louisiana Racing Commission, which regulates Delta Downs, began immediate investigations. A veterinarian gave Landing Officer the once over, finding that despite its near-record win, the horse was barely panting. And in a tell-tale sign, the horse's leggings, which you would expect to be spattered with mud after a one-mile sprint, were remarkably clean.

Jockey Sylvester Carmouche was suspended for the rest of the meet, with allegations he'd hidden in the fog as the horses completed the first lap, then joined them as they circled the track a second time, bolting to the front. Carmouche denied any such thing, claiming he just had a very fast mount. "I didn't know the horse was going that fast," he insisted. "I just wanted to get back safely."

THE AFTERMATH

Louisiana State Police arrested Carmouche, then 31, charging him with felony theft by fraud. A formal inquiry was held, at which Carmouche's lawyer Kenneth Schaffer argued: "He could have passed people in the fog, and they would never have seen him." Officials studied the video of the race and, even allowing for the fog, could not see the number 8 of Landing Officer for much of the run. After weighing up the evidence, the eight man panel voted 7-1 to ban Carmouche for 10 years, ruling he had deliberately cheated to win the race ... even if they weren't 100 percent sure how. "As my mother used to say, I don't know how you spilled the milk, I just know you spilled it," one member of the commission, Jeffrey Kallenberg, said.

"I never did anything wrong in my life," Carmouche protested. "I rode the race, and I won. It ain't right. I know I ain't did it."

Carmouche was reinstated after eight and a half years and rekindled his career. He had some success on Hallowed Dreams, a fine horse that won her first 16 straight races in 1999 and 2000. But Carmouche never quite managed to live down the tag of 'the fog jockey' and the unflattering nickname followed him around for the rest of his time at the track.

ALI REFUSES TO BE DRAFTED, 1966

THE BACKGROUND

The Vietnam War divided the American nation in the 1960s. Starting in 1955 as a conflict between Communist forces in the north and American-backed forces in the south, the war was to last 20 years. By the mid-1960s, thousands of young Americans took to the streets in protest against the war and the draft. One of the highest-profile people among those fighting against the war was a young boxer, then known as Cassius Clay.

In 1964, Clay won the world heavyweight title, defeating Sonny Liston. He joined the Nation of Islam the same year and converted to Sunni Islam in 1965, changing his name to

Ali and his family meeting President Jimmy Carter, years later in 1977.

Muhammad Ali. An outspoken critic of the war, Ali looked set to avoid the draft when he failed the US Armed Forces qualifying test due to his poor writing and spelling skills. But early in 1966, the tests were altered to make them easier; this time Ali passed and was re-classified as 1A. As a result, he became eligible to be drafted into the US Army.

Ali promptly declared he was a conscientious objector and would refuse to serve in the Army. "War is against the teachings of the Holy Qur'an," Ali said. "I'm not trying to dodge the draft. We are not supposed to take part in no wars unless declared by Allah or The Messenger. We don't take part in Christian wars or wars of any unbelievers." Explaining his stance, he added, "I ain't got no quarrel with them Viet Cong; they never called me n****r."

THE SCANDAL

Ali became the poster boy for the opposition to the war. "No, I am not going 10,000 miles to help murder, kill, and burn other people to simply help continue the domination of white slavemasters over dark people the world over. This is the day and age when such evil injustice must come to an end," he thundered. He turned up for his scheduled induction into the U.S. Army in Houston, Texas, in April 1967. A huge crowd gathered outside, many chanting "Don't Go, Don't Go," in support of the popular boxer. He underwent a physical examination and passed. But then three times officials called his name ... and all three times Ali refused to step forward. Warned that he was set to commit a felony punishable by five years in prison and a $10,000 fine, he refused to come forward one last time.

Within hours, the New York State Athletic Commission suspended his boxing licence, stripping him of his title. As word spread, other boxing commissions did the same. Ali and his legal representatives appealed against the draft board's rejection of his application as a conscientious objector. The Justice Department held a hearing into the matter and declared, against a hearing officer's recommendation, that Ali's claim was to be denied. They ruled that Ali did not fall into any of the three basic tests for conscientious objector status. The Appeal Board also denied Ali's application, but, significantly, did not spell out its reasons.

Undeterred, Ali refused to turn up for induction, for which he was tried and convicted. By 1971, the case went as high as the Supreme Court, which decided that because the Appeals Board gave no exact reason for Ali's denial as a conscientious objector, it was impossible to rule on which of the three grounds his application he had been denied on. As such, the conviction was reversed.

THE AFTERMATH

In 1973, President Nixon ended the draft, and the war finally ended two years later, following the withdrawal of American forces in 1975. But the case remains one of the most important in modern US history, shaping and re-defining the meaning of the term 'conscientious objector' While it made him some enemies in the establishment, the case helped affirm Ali as one of the most popular sportsmen the world has seen. His battle against the government at a time when many Americans were questioning the war in Vietnam made him a folk hero. Basketball legend Kareem Abdul-Jabbar said of Ali's battle against the odds, "He gave so many people courage to test the system."

Ali went on to become the only man to win the world heavyweight title three times. He was the key figure as boxing experienced a golden age in the 1970s and 80s, fighting a series of historic bouts against the likes of George Foreman and Joe Frazier. A graceful, talented athlete, he was also a tremendous showman who is among the most famous figures of the 20th century.

He had 61 professional fights, winning 56, 37 by knockout. He retired in 1981 after back-to-back losses to Trevor Berbick and Larry Holmes, but remains one of America's favourite sons.

PARALYMPIC FRAUDS, 2000

THE BACKGROUND

The Paralympic Games were founded in 1960 and were seen as an excellent avenue for athletes with disabilities to compete on the world's largest sporting stage. But officials of the International Paralympic Committee soon found that even disabled athletes could be just as capable and willing as able-bodied athletes to cheat. They were forced to bring in random drug testing and in 1992, at the Barcelona Games, five athletes returned positive results. Concerned at the rise of drug use by some competitors, the IPC also introduced out-of-competition testing in a bid to stamp out illegal drug use.

At the Sydney Paralympics in 2000, no less than nine powerlifters were found to have returned positive results before the competition even began. One powerlifter and one track athletics competitor were also forced to return medals after testing positive to drugs. There were reports of athletes sitting on tacks and sticking themselves with pins. These methods caused them no pain in their paralysed limbs, but made their blood pressure rise and improved performance by up to 15 percent.

The IPC extended the range of the Paralympics in Atlanta in 1996, allowing athletes with a mental disability to compete for the first time. Athletes had to undergo an IQ test to qualify, with only those with an IQ score less than 70 eligible to compete.

THE SCANDAL

Spain proved too good for the competition in basketball, taking the gold medal in convincing style. The Spanish won all three of their preliminary-round games, thumped Poland 97-67 in the semi-final and then outclassed Russia 87-63 in the final to finish in first place.

But soon after the Spaniards were presented with the gold medal, one of their players, Carlos Ribagorda, dropped a bombshell. Ribagorda was actually an undercover journalist and claimed that many members of the Spanish team never underwent medical or mental testing to determined whether they in fact had a disability. The IPC investigated his claims and found that, just as Ribagorda had claimed, the Spanish Paralympic Committee did not conduct the tests.

Ribagorda had joined the team two years before, when invited to take part. He decided to go along with the ruse, then break the story after the Games. He alleged that around 10 of the 12 players in the Spanish squad had no intellectual disability and a lawyer, an engineer and several students were on the team. He also alleged that Spanish athletes, and those of other nationalities, competed in sports including table tennis, track and field and swimming despite having no disabilities. After the scandal broke, an American Paralympic coach went a step further, admitting that many countries allowed players with ADD or dyslexia to compete.

The Russians were subsequently elevated into the gold medal position, with Poland collecting the silver and Portugal the bronze. The disqualification of the Spanish didn't surprise local officials; one Australian commented that several members of the Spanish team would have been good enough to play in the Australian National Basketball League.

THE AFTERMATH

Ribagorda's most damning allegation was that Spanish officials were fully aware of the ruse, warning the basketball team to "slow the rhythm of our play so as not to awaken suspicions". He alleged the Spaniards were desperate for a healthy medal haul in Sydney to increase their chances of securing lucrative sponsorship deals on the home front. Spain enjoyed its most successful Paralympics in Sydney, finishing third on the medal table.

Fernando Martin Vicente, president of the Spanish Federation for Mentally Handicapped Sports, heatedly denied the allegations when they were first raised. "I am completely sure that no fraud has existed. All athletes have undergone the appropriate controls," he said. But when Ribagorda's claims were proven correct, Vicente resigned, declaring, "the process of psychological evaluation is very difficult because there are no amputations nor obvious physical defect. If someone wants to cheat, it's difficult to detect. It's easy to pretend you have little intelligence, but the opposite is difficult."

Rocked by the controversy, which made worldwide headlines, the International Paralympic Committee suspended all sports involving athletes with intellectual disability. As a result of the scandal and the difficulty in evaluating athletes, all events for athletes with learning disabilities were abandoned for the 2004 Paralympic Games in Athens. But in the ensuing years, the International Sports Federation for Persons with an Intellectual Disability began a push to have them re-introduced. The IPC gradually began allowing intellectual disability athletes, but did so with stringent "sports intelligence" testing, and they were allowed to compete again in London in 2012.

ARMSTRONG CONFESSES WEB OF LIES, 2013

THE BACKGROUND

Lance Armstrong is the most famous road cyclist the world has ever known. A seven-time winner of the sport's Holy Grail, the Tour de France, Armstrong was one of the best-known sportsman on the planet before his world came crashing down late in 2012. Originally a triathlete, Armstrong won US national sprint course triathlons in 1989 and 1990 while still

Lance Armstrong, mid-race, in 2002.

a teenager. In 1992, at the age of 21, he turned to professional cycling, joining the Motorola team. He quickly established himself as an elite long-distance competitor and the following year won the world championship, the beginning of a long domination the likes of which the sport had never seen.

In 1996, he was diagnosed with testicular, brain and lung cancer. Six months later, after enduring several surgeries and large doses of chemotherapy, he was declared cured. He founded a cancer charity, the Lance Armstrong Foundation, later called Livestrong, and by early 1998 was back in full training.

He soon proved he had lost nothing of his power, strength and drive, setting records that stunned the cycling world. He won a record seven Tour de France titles and finally retired in 2011, facing – and strongly denying – a US federal government investigation into doping allegations. Armstrong had seen it all before; he had previously been rumoured to have used 'enhancements', but without any firm proof or evidence. As he had done many times before, he hit out at his detractors, pointing out that he had never failed a drug test in his long career.

THE SCANDAL

The USADA (United States Anti-Doping Agency) created worldwide headlines in June 2012, when it formally charged Armstrong with using illicit performance-enhancing drugs. Two months later, it went a step further, banning him for life and stripping him of all titles he had won after August 1998. USADA commented that Armstrong had used "the most sophisticated, professionalised and successful doping program that sport has ever seen". Weeks later, cycling's governing body, UCI (the International Cycling Union), announced it accepted USADA's findings.

Initially, Armstrong stuck to his guns, insisting the punishment was a witch-hunt by his many enemies and rivals. But finally, in a televised interview with former chat show host Oprah Winfrey early in 2013, Armstrong came clean. Winfrey began with a series of 'yes-or-no' questions. Did Armstrong take banned substances? Did that include the banned blood-booster EPO? Did he use blood doping and transfusions? Did he use testosterone, cortisone and human growth hormone? And did he take banned substances or blood dope in all his Tour de France wins? Armstrong answered 'yes' to all five questions. The champion cyclist admitted his guilt in a two-part TV show that went for over four hours. Armstrong admitted he cheated, taking steroids and other drugs, but said he felt no guilt at the time. "I went and looked up the definition of cheat," he said. "And the definition is to gain an advantage on a rival or foe. I didn't view it that way. I viewed it as a level playing field."

THE AFTERMATH

Armstrong refused to implicate any team-mates or officials. "I'm not comfortable talking about other people," he said. "I don't want to accuse anybody." Armstrong admitted that many who had dared to speak out against him, and who he used his power, wealth and influence to silence, would enjoy his downfall. "I deserve this," he told Oprah, more than once. "It's a major flaw, it's a guy who expected to get whatever he wanted and to control every outcome. And it's inexcusable. And when I say there are people who will hear this and never forgive me, I understand that, I do. That defiance, that attitude, that arrogance, you cannot deny it."

Immediately after his confession, Armstrong hinted at an appeal against his lifelong ban, but World Anti-Doping Agency Director General David Howman said that Armstrong would have to start with a full confession, "not talking to a talk-show host".

The confession cost Armstrong lucrative sponsors and forced him to walk away from his cancer charity. He was also stripped of a bronze medal he won at the 2000 Olympics. His words were backed up by WADA president, John Fahey. "He was wrong, he cheated and there was no excuse for what he did," Fahey said.

HARLEQUINS CHEAT WITH FAKE BLOOD, 2009

THE BACKGROUND

In April 2009, English rugby union team Harlequins was involved in a vital quarter-final clash in the Heineken Cup against Irish club Leinster. Harlequins replaced their best goal-kicker, fly-half Nick Evans, early in the game, but a series of injuries saw Harlequins without a regular goal-kicker late in the game. With Leinster holding a slender 6-5 lead, Harlequins were not allowed any more regular replacements. A blood bin rule, however, brought in to permit the replacement of injured players, saw Harlequins winger Tom Williams come off the field with blood oozing from his mouth. Williams winked at team-mates as he was escorted off, a gesture that was captured by a SKY Sports camera, but not broadcast live at the time.

Evans replaced Williams and got an opportunity to snatch a win for Harlequins with a late shot at penalty goal. But the ball sailed wide of the posts, and Leinster hung on for a 6-5 win, knocking Harlequins out of the Cup.

Immediately after the game, Leinster questioned the substitution, but Harlequins' Director of Rugby, Dean Richards, fired back: "You have to know the rules . . . if they [Leinster] don't, it's not my problem. It was almost a last throw of the dice to bring back Nick. I was a bit reluctant but went with it."

THE SCANDAL

Five days after the game, the European Rugby Cup (ERC) launched an investigation into the incident, appointing disciplinary officer Roger O'Connor to interview players and officials from both teams and to examine video footage of the game. After three months of investigating, the ERC found that Williams bit a blood capsule, allegedly at Richards' request. They suspended the winger for 12 months, while clearing Richards, Harlequins doctor Wendy Chapman and physiotherapist Steph Brennan of any wrongdoing. Under intense pressure and the national media spotlight, Richards resigned his role as the director of Harlequins rugby, two weeks after being cleared.

The following week, *The Telegraph* newspaper dropped another bombshell, alleging that Williams had his mouth cut by a club official in an attempt to make the fake injury look real. Some 48 hours after that, Richards was banned for three years, while Brennan was ousted for two years. Williams' ban was reduced from a year to four months after he helped officials in their investigations. The International Rugby Board announced the bans would be worldwide, a move preventing Williams or Richards from getting a job in another rugby-playing country. Harlequins were also fined £258,000, a hefty increase on their original fine of £215,000, half of which was suspended over two years.

THE AFTERMATH

The fallout continued in late August when Harlequins chairman and one of the club's main investors, Charles Jillings, stood down as a director. "We ... acknowledge that we failed to control Dean Richards," Jillings said in a prepared statement. "I trusted Dean. As a result of the board's failure to exercise control, the club cheated. This is totally unacceptable."

Williams told the inquiry that Harlequins had offered him a lucrative contract extension and bonuses if he appealed on only a "limited" basis, thereby not exposing the full extent of the club's cheating and attempted cover-up. Jillings denied this was anything sinister. "I sought a solution, not a cover-up," the chairman said. "The offer of compensation [to Williams] was for damage incurred and was not a bribe or a threat ... I made it clear to Tom that he had cheated and lied and this was no basis for being rewarded."

Dr Chapman was suspended by Britain's General Medical Council for allegedly cutting Williams' lip. She admitted she cut Williams' lip because the player wanted to show he had a "real" injury. Dr Chapman was reinstated in September 2010.

Williams acknowledged his error, but only after the event. "I let down my team-mates and the club's fans and I'll have to live with those actions for the rest of my career," Williams said. "In deciding to come clean and do the right thing, I've tried honestly to rectify this mess and repay the good faith shown in me by my friends and family."

Richards, who returned to coaching with Newcastle Falcons after his three-year ban was served, tried to play down the drama. "I took full responsibility for it," he said. "It was a farcical situation."

After their narrow 6-5 win, Leinster went on to win the Heineken Cup for the first time in the club's history.

BLACK POWER SALUTE, 1968

THE BACKGROUND

In the US, the 1960s were a time of tremendous social unrest and drama. Coming into the Mexico City Olympic Games, an organisation called the Olympic Project for Human Rights, founded by leading sociologist Harry Edwards, pushed for all black athletes to pull out of the Games in protest at the treatment of African-Americans in their own country. OPHR also demanded that South Africa and Rhodesia (now Zimbabwe), two countries with apartheid regimes, be excluded from the Games; that Muhammad Ali be reinstated as world champion, after being stripped of his title for refusing to join the Army; that more African-American professional sports coaches be hired; and that veteran official Avery Brundage resign as head of the IOC.

Only one of the conditions was met, with South Africa and Rhodesia having their invitations to the Games withdrawn, but several athletes decided to support the American Civil Rights Movement in their own way.

THE SCANDAL

On 16 October 1968, African-American Tommie Smith, a former California junior state champion, on scholarship at San Jose State University, won gold in the 200m race in Mexico City, setting a new world record of 20.06 seconds. The silver medal produced a major shock, going to a relatively unknown white Australian, Peter Norman. In third place was another African-American, John Carlos from Harlem in New York.

The trio decided to make a statement when they received their medals that night, and it shook the world. The two Americans received their medals shoeless, wearing black socks, to symbolise black poverty. Smith wore a black scarf around his neck to represent black pride, while Carlos had his tracksuit top open in a show of solidarity with the working class. Carlos also wore a beaded necklace, which he later explained was "for those individuals that were lynched or killed, that no-one said a prayer for".

Norman, an opponent of the racist White Australia policy being practiced in his country at the time, wore an OPHR badge to support his two fellow athletes. As the American national anthem was played immediately after the medal presentation, the two Americans stood with heads bowed, each raising a single black-gloved fist to symbolise black power. Smith later described the gesture as a "human rights salute" rather than a "Black Power salute". The trio were booed off the podium by large sections of the crowd.

The IOC reacted swiftly, declaring the incident a political statement and, as such, contrary to the Olympic spirit. Brundage, the IOC president, demanded the US team punish Smith and Carlos and expel them from the Olympics. Ironically, Brundage had been head of the US Olympic Committee in 1936, when German athletes gave the Nazi salute on the podium.

THE AFTERMATH

The US Olympic Committee initially refused to censure the pair, but when the IOC threatened to ban the whole US team, they relented, and the duo were sent home.

Smith and Carlos returned to a media and public relations storm in America. They were shunned by many of their countrymen and received death threats. Later, Smith went on to play NFL football with the Cincinnati Bengals, while Carlos joined the Philadelphia Eagles. Both have received numerous human rights awards for their actions in the years since – the same actions that were so heavily condemned back in 1968 – including the Arthur Ashe Courage Award in 2008. Both are members of the National Track and Field Hall of Fame and continue to campaign for human rights.

Norman was snubbed by Australian officials and, despite impressive times, never ran for his country at Olympic level again. The US Olympic team invited him to be involved in the 2000 Olympics in Sydney when he was overlooked by Australian organisers. The Australian government has since debated on an apology for Norman in parliament. When he died of a heart attack in 2006, aged 64, both Smith and Carlos flew to his home town of Melbourne for the funeral, where they gave speeches and acted as pallbearers. Norman's nephew, Matthew Norman, produced a moving documentary of his uncle's life and the incident, simply entilted *Salute*, in 2008.

The IOC's own website still struggles to come to terms with the stance taken by the

American duo, stating: "Over and above winning medals, the black American athletes made names for themselves by an act of racial protest."

San Jose University has recognised the historic moment when the athletes made their daring protest with a 22-foot high statue of the medal presentation, while the incident has become a symbol of human rights protest throughout the world.

SOCCER STAR MURDERED AFTER OWN GOAL, 1994

THE BACKGROUND

The Colombian soccer team arrived at the 1994 World Cup in the USA under massive pressure. Allegedly backed by money from infamous drug lord Pablo Escobar, Colombia had built a powerhouse team in the early 1990s and soccer's best ever player, Pele, tipped them to be crowned world champions at the tournament. The national team had close ties to Escobar, and even visited him in jail when he found himself behind bars shortly before the World Cup began. The team was well led by popular defender Andres Escobar (no relation to Pablo), known as 'The Gentleman of Football' because of his reputation for fair play and sportsmanship.

But things didn't go to plan for Colombia. Their goalkeeper had been thrown in jail just before the tournament because of his close association with Pablo Escobar, forcing a late change to the team make-up. The Colombians suffered a shock 3-1 loss to Romania in their opening game and found themselves in a must-win situation against home team the USA in their second. Powerful figures back home were fuming at the loss to Romania after betting heavily on the Colombians. The team received death threats, with an anonymous caller telling officials he would kill the entire team if one player, Jaime Gomez, played against the USA. Gomez was stood down and retired from international football the next day.

In the game itself, midway through the first half, an American player out wide kicked the ball across-field, and Andres Escobar intercepted it. But he only succeeded in deflecting the ball past his goalkeeper into his own net, giving USA a 1-0 lead. The own goal stunned the Colombians, who ultimately lost 2-1, their World Cup dreams shattered.

THE SCANDAL

The Colombians returned home to a hostile reception, with many fans and influential figures believing they had shamed the country. Ten nights after his now infamous own goal, Andres Escobar visited a nightclub in his hometown, Medellin. He returned to his car around 3am, when three men surrounded him. An argument ensued, with the players heckling Escobar about the own goal. Two of the men took out handguns and Escobar was shot six times. One gunman allegedly yelled, each time he pulled the trigger, "Goal . . . goal . . . goal." Escobar was rushed to hospital but died within the hour. His funeral in Medellin drew an estimated crowd of 120,000 people.

Pablo Escobar had been shot dead after getting out of jail several months prior to Andres' death, and many believed that, had he still been alive, no one in Colombia would have had the audacity to kill one of 'his' players.

The boss of world soccer, FIFA general secretary Sepp Blatter, echoed the thoughts of many throughout the world when he declared: "This is the saddest day I have ever witnessed in football." The World Cup was still in progress at the time, with several games observing a minute's silence as a mark of respect. It was never proved that Andres' death was linked to drug lords who lost massive amounts of money on the Colombians' defeat at the World Cup, but those close to him remain convinced it was a major factor.

THE AFTERMATH

Just days before his slaying, Escobar was encouraged by friends and family to write a column for a local newspaper about the own goal and World Cup experience. He wrote a column about his team's below-par performance, finishing with the fateful words: 'Life doesn't end here.'

On the night of Escobar's death, police arrested Humberto Munoz, a bodyguard employed by a local cartel whose bosses included men who lost heavily on the Colombians in the World Cup. The following day, he confessed to firing the shots that killed the soccer star. Despite the fact there was believed to be at least one other gunman, no one else was ever charged with the crime. Munoz was found guilty by a court and sentenced to 43 years behind bars, but was out within 11 years for good behaviour. His release prompted an angry reaction from those close to Andres Escobar. "Frankly, there is no justice in Colombia," Escobar's shattered father Dario said.

Eight years after Escobar's death, a statue was erected in his honour in Medellin. Fans still take his photo to games and he remains a beloved figure in Colombian sport. Many members of the national team never played soccer again after the Escobar tragedy, and Colombia has never qualified for the World Cup since.

NFL SAINTS' BOUNTY BLUES, 2010

THE BACKGROUND

Bounties, in which players are paid bonuses for injuring opponents, are known to have been part of American professional football over the years, even though NFL officials condemn the practice, with many denying its very existence. 'Non-contract bonuses', as the NFL prefers to call them, are technically illegal as they are seen as a way of beating the salary cap. The NFL's collective bargaining agreement with the Players Association bans them, and they are not allowed to be included in player contracts. The NFL reinforces this by sending regular memos to players, agents and teams warning against 'bonuses'. But critics and commentators have long believed that some teams not only pay players bonuses for playing well, but also for hurting opposition players.

The whispers became louder in 2009, when the New Orleans Saints won Super Bowl XLIV. The matter came to a head when the Saints beat the Minnesota Vikings in the NFC Championship game. Vikings quarterback Brett Favre was the victim of several late and dangerous hits during the game, and coach Brad Childress claimed Favre had been deliberately targeted by cheap shots. In the off season, an anonymous player told the NFL that Saints had targeted both Favre and Arizona quarterback Kurt Warner a week earlier as part of a wide-ranging bounty program allegedly initiated by Saints' defensive coordinator Gregg Williams.

THE SCANDAL

The NFL began investigating Saints in 2010 after several more instances of rival quarterbacks and key players being singled out for special attention. The investigation stalled initially, with

Saints players denying all accusations. But late in the 2011 season, the NFL received "significant and credible" new information that the bounty system was rife within the Saints, with up to 20 players involved. In March 2012, the NFL declared it had solid proof that the Saints had been using a bounty system since 2009 under Williams, who joined the team the same year. The NFL claimed the players and Williams put their own money into a pot and then paid out cash bonuses every week. Extra cash – around $1000 – was paid if an opposition player was significantly hurt or could take no further part in a game. The payments increased during playoffs and other big games. It was also revealed that Saints linebacker Jonathan Vilma made an offer of $10,000 to any player who could knock Favre out in the NFC Championship game. Seattle quarterback Matt Hasselbeck was revealed as another target in the 2011 wild-card playoff against Saints, with a bounty placed on his head. As well as getting bonuses, players were fined for basic errors.

THE AFTERMATH

NFL officials sent the full results of their findings to all 32 teams. They declared that Saints head coach Sean Payton knew about the scheme and attempted to cover it up when the NFL launched its investigation. Team owner Tom Benson was informed of the findings by the NFL and ordered Payton and Saints' general manager, Mickey Loomis, to end it immediately. They did not do so initially and were slammed by the NFL for "conduct detrimental" to the game.

Several Saints players testified before a federal judge in New Orleans in 2012 that NFL commissioner Roger Goodell's accusations were false. But the evidence continued to mount. Several Washington Redskins players revealed to the *Washington Post* that Williams operated a similar bounty system when he was the team's defensive coordinator from 2004 to 2007. Buffalo Bills players came out after that, claiming another bounty scheme when Williams was head coach in 2001–03.

Williams eventually left the Saints for a job in St Louis, but was hauled before the NFL in February 2012. After initially denying any involvement, he admitted his part in the scheme, calling it a "terrible mistake" in a prepared statement. Goodell slammed the team, declaring that it was "particularly disturbing" that Saints players would try to injure rival players. Payton and Loomis also came clean, taking responsibility for not stopping the scheme.

The NFL handed out heavy penalties. Williams was suspended indefinitely; Payton ousted for the entire 2012 season; and Loomis barred from the first eight games of 2012. Vilma, who the NFL concluded was one of the scheme's ringleaders, was rubbed out for the entire 2012 season as well, the heaviest suspension for a player in modern day NFL history.

MIRACLE IN THE ANDES, 1972

THE BACKGROUND

In October 1972, a group of Uruguayan rugby union players set out on a plane trip to Chile for a game. Some 40 passengers aboard a twin turboprop plane had to spend a night in Mendoza, Argentina, due to inclement weather. The next day, they set out again, but could not fly in a straight line because of the conditions. Heading south, parallel to the Andes, they crossed through a low pass in the mountains before heading to the Chilean city of Santiago. But as they descended the pass was covered by clouds, and strong headwinds had placed them further from Santiago than the pilots thought.

The plane crashed into a mountain nearly 14,000 feet above sea level, clipping a second mountain before coming to rest in a snow bank. Twelve people died in the crash and another five perished within the first 24 hours from their injuries. Others suffered broken bones and, with no proper medical supplies, endured great pain.

Once the plane did not arrive, search parties from three different countries began combing the mountains. But the wreckage was white, blending in with the snow, and after eight days the search was cancelled, the passengers all presumed dead. The survivors then faced a new peril – starvation. At the time of the crash, they had a few candy bars and snacks but these soon dwindled. As days became weeks, they were faced with a horrible choice to make.

THE SCANDAL

They tried everything – eating strips of leather torn from luggage, and the seat cushions, but these could not give them any sustenance. The plane crashed at such a height that there were no natural vegetation or animals they could consume.

Weak and numbed by the cold, the survivors made the chilling decision to eat the flesh of their dead team-mates. One of the leaders of the group, Nando Parrado, explained, "I knew those bodies represented our only chance of survival." Several players resisted the urge to indulge in cannibalism, but eventually relented as they realised this represented their lone hope. Many among the group were devout Roman Catholics and while the church condemned such actions, they equated eating their friends and loved ones as similar to the act of Holy Communion.

On 29 October, 16 days after the crash, the remaining survivors were sleeping in the fuselage of the plane when it was struck by an avalanche. The mass of snow killed eight more people, including the last surviving woman, Liliana Methol. With no hope of being rescued, the remaining survivors realised their only way of staying alive was to attempt to return to civilisation themselves. But that would involve a long and hazardous journey through the snow-covered mountains. After several aborted attempts, three members of the group, including Parrado, set out on 12 December, two months after the crash.

THE AFTERMATH

The trio walked for five days, unsure of their location or exactly where they were headed, before seeing a man on a horse in the distance. They attempted to attract his attention, but he was on the far side of a fast-flowing river. Eventually he spotted the three hapless men and shouted across the river that he would bring rescuers the following day. The man, a Chilean *arriero* (men who use pack animals to transport goods) was true to his word. Meanwhile, two rescue helicopters set off from Santiago to look for the remaining group, still at the wreckage of the plane. The group was finally rescued on the afternoon of 22 December 1972. There were 16 survivors in all. They were taken to hospital suffering from a multitude of problems, including dehydration, frostbite, broken bones, malnutrition and altitude sickness.

The world's media flocked to Chile to tell the story of the incredible survival and, at first, the players attempted to hide the truth about what they had to do to survive. They initially said they ate cheese they carried on them to survive, and planned to tell their loved ones the true stories at a later time. But word leaked out that the players resorted to cannibalism to survive, creating a storm that made front-page headlines around the globe.

The players were disillusioned by the publicity and interest in the means that led to their survival. "Shortly after our rescue, officials of the Catholic Church announced that according to church doctrine, we had committed no sin by eating the flesh of the dead," Parrado wrote years later. "They told the world that the sin would have been to allow ourselves to die. More satisfying for me was the fact that many of the parents of the boys who died had publicly expressed their support for us, telling the world they understood and accepted what we had done to survive … despite these gestures, many news reports focused on the matter of our diet, in reckless and exploitive ways. Some newspapers ran lurid headlines above grisly front-page photos."

Several books and documentary films have been produced about the incident, now known as 'Miracle in the Andes'.

PROTESTING VANDALS RUIN CRICKET TEST, 1975

THE BACKGROUND

George Davis was convicted of armed robbery in England in 1975, after the payroll of the London Electricity Board was stolen from the corporation's offices the previous year. The robbery was an elaborate scheme worthy of a movie, with a dramatic car chase involving a host of vehicles, a shootout and injuries to both police and the robbers. Davis was arrested some time after the raid. Several blood samples were found at the crime scene, which became a major part of the prosecution's case against him. Four men were arrested and accused of the robbery, but Davis was the only man the jury convicted.

There were major doubts about his conviction, however, with the blood samples failing to match Davis' blood, or that of the other three men accused of the crime. Davis' lawyers also argued that he would never have been committed to stand trial in the first place from the lower courts had the blood test results been made public at that time. The results were allegedly suppressed and this enraged Davis' many supporters.

Five police officers also said they saw Davis break into the offices, including two who had been in an unmarked car outside. But one officer recanted part of his testimony, and Davis had an alibi; witnesses said he was working as a taxi driver at the time.

THE SCANDAL

Davis' cause attracted many supporters and they began a vocal and very public campaign to have him released after he was sentenced to 20 years in jail at the Albany Prison on the Isle of Wight. 'Free George Davis' graffiti appeared on public buildings throughout Great Britain.

In 1975, soon after Davis began his jail term, Australia was involved in an epic cricket match against Great Britain in the Third Test at the Headingley ground in Leeds. The game was delicately poised going into the final day, with Australia chasing a mammoth target of 445 to win the game. But on the night before the last day's play, several Davis supporters climbed the fence at the oval and snuck onto the field. The pitch was covered by large tarpaulins, but they burrowed under these and dug large holes in the wicket, into which they poured oil. The sabotage was not discovered until the next morning, when the head groundsman, George Cawthray, and his team were preparing the pitch for what they believed would be a gripping final day. "When I first saw the damage it did not sink in," Cawthray said. "I was amazed. I thought I should be able to repair the holes but it was the oil that did the damage."

The game was abandoned and declared a draw, robbing England of the chance to win back the Ashes trophy and seeing Australia taking the series by one game to nil, with three Tests drawn. Ironically, heavy rain began midway through the final day, so it would have been abandoned anyway due to the weather. After police investigations, four people were charged for vandalism. Three of the suspects received suspended sentences but one, Peter Chappell (no relation to the Australian cricketing brothers), was sentenced to 18 months in jail.

THE AFTERMATH

Davis continued to receive great support – musician Roger Daltrey of The Who appeared at a concert wearing a t-shirt that read: 'George Davis is innocent'. Pop sensations Duran Duran also made reference to him in one of their songs. In December 1975, the British Court of Appeal decided not to overturn Davis' criminal conviction, but five months later, the Home Secretary, Roy Jenkins, reviewed the case and recommended his release. Davis was set free by Exercise of the Royal Prerogative of Mercy, following doubts over the evidence that helped convict him.

Two years later, in 1978, Davis was again jailed after pleading guilty to a 1977 bank robbery. He was released in 1984, but sent to jail again in 1987, convicted of attempting to rob a mail train. After his third stint in jail, Davis went straight, marrying the daughter of a London police inspector and working as a courier driver. He attempted to fully clear his name on the 1974 robbery, a charge which was never quashed, even when he was released, in a trial in 2007. Four years later, the Court of Appeal finally sided with Davis and he won his appeal against the 1975 conviction.

Davis, aged 70 at the time, punched the air with joy in a case that again made national headlines. "It should not have taken 36 long years for me to be able to stand here like this," he told a massive media contingent.

NAZI GENDER BENDER EXPOSURE, 1938

THE BACKGROUND

There was something very unusual about Dora Ratjen from the day she was born. The midwife announced to her father, moments after her birth in the German town of Erichshof in 1918, that she was a boy ... but then five minutes later changed her mind, declaring Dora a girl.

Dora's genitalia were ambiguous and this led to her being confused for much of her life. Her parents brought her up as a female, dressing her in girls' clothes, but Dora felt she was more male than anything. Years later, she admitted, "From the age of 10 or 11, I started to realise I wasn't female, but male. I never asked my parents why I had to wear women's clothes

German athlete Dora Ratjen competing in the high jump.

even though I was male."

Although shy and awkward, Dora found an outlet that gained her popularity – sport. She joined the Kormet Bremen Athletic Club and became an excellent high jumper, winning several national titles. At 15, she won the regional championship of Lower Saxony. After leaving school, she continued to jump while working as a packer in a tobacco factory, surrounded by women who found her odd and aloof.

THE SCANDAL

Legend has it that the Nazis realised Dora was a man, but pushed her to compete in the 1936 Olympics anyway, as a woman. They did so to avoid embarrassing Hitler and his cronies by having a Jewish German woman, Gretel Bergmann, win a gold medal at the 1936 Olympics. Bergmann had been favoured to win gold, but was barred by the Nazis from competing shortly before the Games began. In a recent interview, Bergmann claimed the Nazis knew Dora was male, even if she and her fellow competitors did not. "I never had any suspicions, not even once," Bergmann said. "In the communal showers we wondered why she never showed herself naked ... but no one knew or noticed anything different about her sexuality."

The incident was dramatised in a 2009 movie, *Berlin 36*, but some historians believe the Nazis were unaware that Dora was in fact a man. With Bergmann banished, Dora was a great chance for a medal, but finished fourth. The following year, however, she finished in first place at the European Athletics Championships with a leap of 1.63 metres.

On a train ride from Vienna to Cologne in 1938, the conductor went to police, claiming a passenger was "a man dressed as a woman". The police detained Dora and the local constable was convinced she was a man, threatening to examine her himself. Eventually he called a doctor, who examined her, and declared she was in fact a man, although he added that the genitalia were odd. Dora was arrested and mug shots were taken. She was charged on suspicion of fraud against Hitler's Third Reich. She was then sent to a sports sanitarium, where doctors were stumped by her physical characteristics.

THE AFTERMATH

The Nazis considered charging Dora with a crime and began criminal proceedings, but these were dropped in March 1939, when the public prosecutor declared: "Fraud cannot be deemed to have taken place because there was no intention to reap financial reward."

Dora promised she would cease competing in athletics as a female to appease the authorities, essentially ending her career at the age of 21. Her gold medal from the European Athletic Championships the previous year was taken back, and her name struck from the records. The registry office in her hometown amended her birth certificate, changing her from a woman to a man. Her father Heinrich Ratjen still regarded her as a woman but, under pressure from the authorities, wrote a letter to the local police chief requesting that they "change the child's first name to Heinrich".

Dora, or Heinrich as he was now known, was issued with new identity papers and moved to Hanover, where he survived the carnage of World War II. He worked in his parents' bar and took over the licence after their deaths, but refused all interview requests. Finally, in 1966, *TIME* magazine wrote a story about Heinrich in which it was alleged he had been forced by the Nazis to pose as a woman in an attempt to win a gold medal for Germany in the 1936 Olympics.

He died in Bremen in 2008, aged 90. The case is still the subject of intense debate among scientists and gender researchers.

JORDAN DEFECTS TO BASEBALL, 1994

THE BACKGROUND

Michael Jordan is universally regarded as one of the best basketball players of all time. His talents first came to light at the University of North Carolina, where he led the Tar Heels to the national championship in 1982. Two years later, he joined the Chicago Bulls and quickly established himself as one of the NBA's true showman. A point-scoring freak, Jordan's ability to leap to amazing heights, perform spectacular slam dunks and athleticism around the court saw him dubbed "Air Jordan". Jordan was the star of the Bulls' memorable three consecutive titles in 1991, 1992 and 1993, but at the end of the 1993 season, the pressure of being the face of the game was beginning to tell.

Late in 1993, Jordan stunned the game by announcing his retirement. But a bigger shock was still to come. Jordan's father James had been murdered earlier that year, shot by two teenagers at a highway rest area in North Carolina. They were caught and convicted and both handed life terms in prison. James Jordan's dream had always been for his son to play Major League Baseball. So Jordan signed with the Chicago White Sox and was assigned to play in the minor leagues. He was raw and out of his depth, but the sporting world watched with fascination as Jordan attempted to take on this new challenge.

THE SCANDAL

Jordan's arrival at spring training in March 1994 was akin to a circus. Hundreds of TV cameras, photographers and journalists followed his every move and his foray into a rival sport drew plenty of critics. After watching him go through his paces, the world's highest selling sports magazine, *Sports Illustrated*, ran a cover story with the words: "Bag It, Michael." *Sun Times* sports writer Jay Mariotti was also unimpressed by what he saw of Jordan on the diamond: "This was classic Reinsdorfian sham [a reference to Bulls chairman Jerry Reinsdorf], an insult to the trained eye and the sophisticated sports fan, nothing but a bored retireee struggling to put good wood on grooved 55mph lollipops." Peter Vecsey of *The New York Post* added, "Who really cares if Jordan eventually becomes one of 600 or so Major League players? We're talking Michael Jordan here, one of the greatest figures in the history of sports and the NBA's best player of all time, permitting himself to be transformed into nothing more than a curiosity."

There were also many who were prepared to believe that the White Sox were cashing in on Jordan's fame at the expense of the game (and of young players legitimately trying to make a career in baseball). "Jordan gets special treatment because he sells tickets. His signing is an insult to every player who came up through the minor leagues," said Mel Antonen of *USA Today*.

Baseball broadcaster and former MLB catcher Tim McCarver put it even more bluntly: "His chances aren't one in a million ... The odds are one in a billion. That's nine zeros. I say he has no chance."

Jordan played for the Birmingham Barons and the team played to sellout crowds and massive TV coverage for every game.

THE AFTERMATH

Jordan was not a great player early on, but worked hard and got better. In the 1994 season, he batted .202, hit three home runs, 51 runs batted in and 30 stolen bases, with 11 errors. He then joined the Scottsdale Scorpions in the Arizona Fall League, raising his average to .252. He quit baseball in 1995, rejoining the Bulls and inspiring them to three more NBA championships. He then retired again in 1999, before a two-season comeback in 2001–03 with the Washington Wizards.

Film director Ron Shelton produced a TV documentary on Jordan's baseball experiment and came to believe that the star's switch gave him the motivation to return to basketball as a changed man. "I think Jordan learned," Shelton said. "As an NBA superstar, he'd taken it for granted; then he saw how hard it was to be a professional athlete, these guys struggling in the minor leagues. And these were very, very good athletes. He learned to appreciate what he had."

Michael Jordan's baseball shirt remains the most popular item in the Birmingham Barons' souvenir shop.

WAR IN HUNGARY, WAR IN THE WATER, 1956

THE BACKGROUND

In 1956, the eyes of the world were on Hungary. A dramatic people's uprising against the country's Russian rulers saw street battles and deaths on both sides as the Cold War exploded. With the Melbourne Olympics just weeks away, Hungary's world champion water polo team was isolated in a training camp high above the capital city of Budapest, where they could hear gunfire and see smoke, but were basically kept in the dark. What further enraged the Hungarians was that the Russian team, eager to end the Hungarians' domination of the sport, allegedly attended Hungarian training sessions earlier in 1956, taking notes and duplicating the local team's tactics. "They wrote down everything we did," Hungarian star Istvan Hevesi said. "The next day they did the same thing. They copied us."

Only days before the Games, the Hungarians were not even sure if they would be able to defend their Olympic gold medal in Melbourne, as several countries pulled out of the Games as a result of the Russian invasion. But the decision was made to push ahead and the Hungarians began the long journey to Australia. When they arrived, they were able to read news reports of the conflict and came to realise their beloved homeland was in ruins. Thousands were dead, with Russian tanks rolling through the streets of Budapest. The Hungarians considered withdrawing from the Games, but decided to play on in an attempt to fight for Hungary's freedom. They breezed through the opening rounds of the tournament, before fate drew them against Russia in the semi-final.

THE SCANDAL

A capacity crowd of over 5,000 attended the match, booing and heckling the Russians from the outset. The Hungarians' plan was not to start the fights, even though they were enraged at Russia's invasion of their homeland. The violence began almost from the start, with players punching, elbowing and kicking each other. "We were yelling at them, 'You dirty bastards ... you come over here and bomb our country.' They were calling us traitors. There was fighting above the water and fighting beneath the water," recalled Hungarian star Ervin Zador.

Five players were ejected from the game – three Russians and two Hungarians. Playing as if their lives depended on it, the Hungarians led 4-0 late in the game. With two minutes to play, the game exploded when Russia's Valentin Prokopov smashed Zador in the face in an off-the-ball incident. Underwater shots show Zador reel from the blow, his cheek split open, blood pouring into the pool. "He tried to punch me out ... I felt warm blood pouring down," Zador recalled. His face badly cut, Zador was taken from the pool and it's then that things really got ugly. The crowd, already incensed, were horrified at the sight of the bloodied Hungarian and charged at the pool, attempting to jump the barricades and attack the Russian players. Police held them back, as missiles were thrown and fists raised at the Russians. The referee, wisely, ended the game prematurely, declaring Hungary the winners.

THE AFTERMATH

The Hungarians advanced to the final as a result, and beat Yugoslavia 2-1 for back-to-back gold medals. Zador, however, was forced to sit out the game with his injuries. Pictures of Zador with blood pouring down his face were run on the front pages of newspapers worldwide and became a symbol of brave Hungarian resistance against the Russian invader. In their homeland, the news of the gold medal was greeted with tears and pride by the Hungarian freedom fighters as they battled the Russian tanks in the streets.

Many of the Hungarian Olympians never returned home, defecting to live out their lives in Australia or the USA. Zador moved to San Francisco, where he became a swimming coach. In the late 1960s, he coached promising young swimmer Mark Spitz to considerable success. When Hollywood legend Quentin Tarantino made a documentary, *Freedom's Fury*, about the famous water polo match 50 years later in 2006, Spitz was the narrator. Surviving members of the two teams had an emotional reunion to mark the anniversary in Budapest.

Hungary finally gained its freedom from Russia in 1989, but the memory of the 1956 revolution, which cost around 3,000 lives, remains part of the country's folklore. In a moving ceremony in 1989, many of the victims of the 1956 revolution, who'd been executed and dumped in unmarked graves, were reburied before huge crowds in Budapest.

CRICKET COACH'S SUSPICIOUS DEATH, 2007

THE BACKGROUND

Bob Woolmer was born to play cricket. His father Clarence was a top cricketer in India and Woolmer was born, in 1948, right across the road from the local cricket ground in the Indian city of Kanpur. His parents sent him to school in England, the home of the game, where he quickly established himself as all-rounder of considerable talent.

He made his debut for Kent in county cricket at just 20 and was selected to play for England at the age of 27 in 1975. He played 19 Tests and scored three centuries, and was also a handy medium pace bowler. His ability to both bat and bowl made him an integral part of the England team when one-day international cricket began in the early 1970s.

While he was a class player, coaching was Woolmer's great talent, and he ran a cricket school that achieved fine results. After retiring in 1984, he moved to South Africa and coached at junior level. Back in England in 1987, he coached Warwickshire, before being appointed South African national coach in 1994. After a slow start, South Africa thrived under his progressive methods in both Tests and one-day internationals. He was among the first coaches to bring computer technology into cricket, helping take the game into a new scientific era. He resigned after the 1999 World Cup and after another stint at Warwickshire, was appointed coach of Pakistan in 2004, after the sacking of the controversial Javed Miandad.

THE SCANDAL

In March 2007, during the World Cup in the West Indies, Woolmer was found dead in his hotel room in Kingston, Jamaica. Tributes poured in from throughout the cricket world, in memory of one of the game's great innovators. Woolmer was just 58.

After initially declaring he had died of a heart attack, Jamaican police launched a murder investigation. They claimed that the former star may have been strangled and that Pakistan's shock loss to Ireland in the World Cup could have given an upset fan the motivation to kill him. "The pathologist's report states that Mr Woolmer's death was due to asphyxiation as a result of manual strangulation," a police spokesman said. There was further speculation that match-fixing groups may have been involved, with several scandals involving match-fixing syndicates having emerged in world cricket at the time.

Some called for the World Cup to be called off; others wanted it dedicated to Woolmer's memory. Pakistan players were also questioned, after it was revealed Woomer had resigned as national coach shortly before his death and had been planning to write a 'tell-all' book about his time as Pakistan coach. Players underwent questioning, fingerprinting and DNA testing, with players and officials angered at the insinuation they may have been involved.

Police examined Woomer's laptop and found nothing related to match-fixing; they also tested his last meal before ruling out that he was poisoned. They launched a search for three mystery men they believed were involved in the death.

THE AFTERMATH

In the weeks after Woolmer's death, pressure from Pakistan to solve the case increased. The Pakistani government offered to send a three-man delegation to Jamaica to help in the investigation, and three detectives from England's Scotland Yard joined the case.

On 1 April, two weeks after his death, a memorial service in Lahore drew over 400 people, including most of the Pakistan team. Woolmer's widow, Gill, confirmed her husband had been planning a book, but said it would never be published. "If it is going to upset people, it is not worth publishing," she said.

Investigations continued in the following weeks, with speculation arising that Woolmer may have been poisoned before being strangled. The Ireland squad that beat Pakistan were subsequently interviewed and sent for DNA testing, ruling them out as suspects. Three weeks after the funeral, Jamaican police finally agree to release the body so it could be buried by the family in South Africa.

In May, Jamaican police insisted they had credible evidence that Woolmer was murdered, while Pakistani investigators declared he had died of natural causes. By June, the Scotland Yard detectives decided Woolmer's death was not suspicious and Jamaican police changed their stance, stating he had not been murdered. The pathologist who conducted the post mortem, Dr Ere Seshaiah, disagreed. "I am sticking to my findings . . . he was murdered," Dr Seshaiah said.

Cricket officials declared the match-fixing allegations had "unnecessarily tarnished" the game; these claims and murder were officially ruled out. But after the confusing media storm, many among the public still wonder if there could have been more to Woolmer's death than met the eye.

JIMMY GAULD SOCCER FIX CONFESSION, 1964

THE BACKGROUND

Jimmy Gauld was a colourful soccer player in Britain in the 1950s. Born in Aberdeen in 1929, he played for Scotland as a boy and began his career at Aberdeen as a teenager. But he failed to make the top team and after short stints at Huntley and Elgin City, he rose to prominence at Waterford in 1954. In his lone season with the club, the talented inside forward bagged 30 goals, making him top scorer in the entire League of Ireland. That attracted the attention of the rich English clubs, and after receiving several offers, he moved to Charlton Athletic the following year. He had stints at Everton and Plymouth Argyle, before Swindon Town signed him in 1959 for a then-club-record transfer fee. A football nomad, who played for eight teams in his 13 seasons of professional football, he then moved to St Johnstone before a badly broken leg ended his career when he was playing for Mansfield Town in 1961.

THE SCANDAL

In 1964, Gauld went to the *Sunday People* newspaper, claiming he had a story that would shock the sporting world. In desperate need of money, Gauld sold his story to the paper for £7,000, and it lived up to his prediction.

Gauld admitted to the paper he had been involved in match-fixing for several years and had enticed a group of players to fix matches and bet against their own teams. He had secretly taped conversations in his car with players to back up his allegations. He revealed that he approached David Layne, a former team-mate at Swindon Town, who was then playing for Sheffield Wednesday, before a match against Ipswich Town in 1962. Gauld encouraged Layne to ensure Wednesday lost the game, and allegedly got team-mates Peter Swan and Tony Kay to do likewise. The three all allegedly bet against their team to win the game. Ipswich Town, who were favourites anyway, ultimately won the game 2-0.

Police swooped after the story was published and charged all four with conspiracy. The matter went to court the following year, where the four were given varying jail terms. The judge made it clear that he regarded Gauld as the ringleader of the group, giving him the heaviest jail term, four years. Upon their release, they received a further blow, with all being banned from any involvement in English football for life.

THE AFTERMATH

Further investigations revealed that Gauld had enticed other players to gamble on matches, but the full extent of his corruption may never be known. Four Mansfield Town players were also found guilty of colluding in the scam in a different game and also jailed. The affair ruined the lives of many of those involved, who were not even allowed to watch their children play junior football matches. "When I'm dead, it will still rise up from the grave," said Peter Swan, who allegedly bet a mere £50 on the crooked outcome, in an interview years later. Swan received four months for his role in the sting and came to believe that corruption in the game was rife at the time. "I'm sure there have been bent referees," he added. "Back in our time there was a lot of talk about it going on in the lower leagues. We were scapegoats but they had to make an example out of us because it was that rife ... We have asked ourselves many times why we did it ... what fools we were."

Swan, who at his peak was rated one of the world's best centre halves and played for England 19 times, admitted to betting on Ipswich Town but insists he and his team-mates did not "throw" the game. "We lost fair and square," he insisted. "But I still don't know what I'd have done if we were winning. It would have been easy for me to give away a penalty or score an own goal. Who knows?"

After seven long years, the English Football Association showed mercy to some of the players, lifting the life bans. Swan returned to Sheffield Wednesday, but by this time was in his mid 30s and past his best. Layne also rejoined Sheffield Wednesday, while Kay never played top-flight football again. Gauld also had no further association with the game, with his now infamous sting becoming the subject of a 1997 British TV movie, *The Fix*.

'BUSBY'S BABES' AIR DISASTER, 1958

THE BACKGROUND

Manchester United were the glamour team of English soccer in the 1950s. Known as 'Busby's Babes', named after manager Matt Busby, the team was full of star power and played to packed houses. In the 1957 season, they were chasing an unprecedented league, FA Cup and European Cup treble.

'Busby's Babes' disembarking an airplane in 1955.

In December 1957, they played a European Cup match against Dukia Prague, losing the game but winning on aggregate. Fog prevented them from flying back to Manchester, forcing them to undergo a long plane, ferry and train trip leading into a game against Birmingham three days later, in which they were weary and only managed a 3-3 draw. The experience concerned United officials who made the fateful decision to charter their own plane, owned by British European Airways, for their next away game, to be held in Belgrade against Red Star on 5 February 1958.

The trip was made in heavy fog and snow, creating poor visibility. A scheduled refuelling stop in Munich saw a risky landing, with visibility so poor that the airport engineer only realised the plane had landed when it taxied onto the airport apron. United drew the game 3-3, but won a spot in the semi-finals on aggregate, having won the first leg 2-1 at their home ground, Old Trafford. The players enjoyed a cocktail party at the British Embassy after the game before heading home the next day.

Their departure from Belgrade, in warm sunshine, was delayed an hour when star player Johnny Berry lost his passport. At 1.15pm, they landed in Munich for another refuelling stop. The plane was a six-year old Airspeed Ambassador 2, the pilots both World War II veterans. Snow was falling when the plane landed in Munich, with several players throwing snowballs at refuelling staff.

THE SCANDAL

The plane was given the 'all clear' to take off, but abandoned the first attempt when the pilots noticed a pressure gauge fluctuating. Three minutes later, they attempted a second take-off, only to abort again. This time, the reason given was that the engines "over-accelerated". The players and officials got off the plane and returned to the airport lounge.

With heavy snow now falling, the players expected to be stuck in Munich for the night. But 15 minutes later, the pilots decided to attempt a third take-off. The players were said to be sceptical, with several even moving to the back of the plane, believing it would improve their chances of survival in a crash.

The plane began to accelerate, but didn't work up the necessary speed to leave the ground as it accelerated. It spun off the end of the runway, crashing into a fence and then across a road. The port wing tore off, hitting a nearby house. The fuselage smashed into a hut that was filled with tyres and fuel, causing a massive explosion and fire.

The captain, James Thain, instructed his crew to give the order to evacuate. The two stewardesses escaped through an emergency window in the galley, followed by Bill Rodgers, the radio operator. Some players were already dead, others dazed, attempting to escape the inferno as the plane went up in flames.

THE AFTERMATH

Eight Manchester United players were among the 23 people who died at the crash scene or at hospital in the days that followed; two more never played again as a result of their injuries. Some 21 others survived the inferno. The bodies of the dead were flown home, spending the night in the Old Trafford gym before being collected by their families. Manager Matt Busby spent over two months in hospital before being discharged. His condition was so grave that a priest twice read him the last rites. Busby eventually recovered and considered walking away from the game but, on the insistence of his wife, returned to United the following year.

Pilot error was initially blamed for the crash, before an investigation found that the build-up of slush and snow on the runway prevented the plane from being able to reach flying speed and caused the crash. Despite this, German authorities took legal action against Captain Thain, claiming he failed to de-ice the wings before take-off. In 1968, Thain was finally cleared. He left British European Airways after the crash and retired to run a poultry farm in the English countryside, before dying in 1975 from a heart attack.

Having lost so many star players, Manchester United struggled on the field for several years after the crash, but in 1967–68 they finally won the European Cup with a new generation of 'Busby's Babes'. Memorials to the victims of the crash are found at both Munich and Old Trafford.

COLTS SKIP TOWN, 1984

THE BACKGROUND

The Colts had been the pride of Baltimore since their inception in 1953, winning three NFL championships and a Super Bowl in 1970, as well as producing a string of star players, most notably quarterback Johnny Unitas. But their home field, Memorial Stadium, was considered outdated and inadequate as far back as the 1960s.

The first signs of tension between the Colts and the city of Baltimore came in 1969, when Baltimore declared it would seek a substantial rental increase from both the Colts and the Orioles, the city's major league baseball club. Carroll Rosenbloom, then the Colts' owner, slammed the city, declaring he would find an alternative venue if the stadium was not updated.

Rosenbloom sold the Colts to millionaire businessman Robert Irsay in 1972 for around $19 million, and Irsay continued where Rosenbloom left off in the battle with city authorities. The previous year, Baltimore mayor William Schaefer had authorised a report into Memorial Stadium and the results were scathing – thousands of seats had poor views, others had no back support, while office facilities for the Colts and Orioles were criticised as well below par. The report also said the bathrooms, parking and other facilities for fans were inadequate. City officials decided to build a new stadium at the Inner Harbor district, dubbed the Baltodome. But the state legislature knocked the expensive proposal on the head and Irsay began shopping his team around. He spoke to the cities of Phoenix, Arizona, and Indianapolis, Indiana, as well as several others. In 1980, Irsay requested a $25 million upgrade of Memorial Park, but talks again broke down.

THE SCANDAL

Irsay continually denied the possibility of moving to Indianapolis, but a visit to the city, and the new Hoosier Dome Stadium that Indiana was building for an NFL team, only fuelled the fire. Sensing the danger, the Maryland legislature stepped in on 27 March 1984, passing a bill that gave Baltimore the right to seize control of the team by eminent domain. To Irsay, this was like a red rag to a bull. As Colts' legal counsel Michael Chernoff later declared, "They not only threw down the gauntlet, but they put a gun to his head and cocked it and asked, 'Want to see if it's loaded?' They forced him to make a decision that day."

The following day, Irsay called Indianapolis government officials seeking urgent negotiations before Maryland's other legislative chamber, the House of Delegates, could pass the same bill. Indianapolis jumped at the opportunity, throwing in a $12.5 million loan, lavish training complex and use of the brand new stadium at Irsay. The deal was hurriedly agreed on, and in the early hours of 29 March, 15 moving trucks were sent to the Colts' training complex at Owings Mills, Maryland. Fearing the city would take control of the team, Irsay ordered the movers to work through the night and by 10am the Colts were out of Baltimore. Each of the 15 Mayflower trucks took a different route to Indiana in a bid to confuse police, who Irsay feared would put a stop to the move.

As the trucks crossed the Indiana State border, each was escorted to Indianapolis by Indiana State Police cruisers. Later the same day, the Maryland House of Delegates signed the Eminent Domain bill.

THE AFTERMATH

The Baltimore public was devastated, feeling betrayed and broken-hearted at losing their beloved football team. The fighting spirit became symbolised by the Baltimore Colts Marching Band, which continued to play around the country despite their football team abandoning the fans. Lawsuits were filed, but a peace agreement was reached when the Colts agreed to endorse a new NFL team for Baltimore in 1986. But many Colts veterans, most notably the legendary Unitas, refused to acknowledge the 'new' Colts. Unitas insisted that he only be called a Baltimore Colt until the day he died in 2002.

In 1995, the Cleveland Browns decided to relocate to Baltimore. But they did so only after striking an agreement with the NFL that the Browns' name, colors and history would stay in Ohio. Owner Art Modell took his players and coaching staff to Baltimore on 1996, and hoped to name the team the Baltimore Colts once again. But, despite an offer of $5 million to the Irsay family, they were turned down. Fans voted on a new name, with the Baltimore Ravens born that year. Ironically, the Ravens played out of Memorial Stadium (the Colts' home field and the source of the original breakaway from the city) for their first two seasons before moving to a new stadium, Camden Yards, in 1998. The Baltimore Ravens won the Super Bowl in 2000, cheered on by many of the Colts' old fans, and plenty of new ones as well.

SELES' ON-COURT STABBING, 1993

THE BACKGROUND

Monica Seles was a tennis child prodigy. Born in Yugoslavia in 1973, she was coached in her early career by her father, Karoly, and won Miami Florida's Orange Bowl tournament at age 11 in 1985. That earned her a place at the famed Nick Bolletieri Tennis Academy, where she honed her skills for the next two years, perfecting her two-handed backhand and forehand play.

She made her debut on the pro tour at just 14 in 1988 and joined the WTA Pro Tour the following year. She won her maiden title at Houston in 1989, beating the legendary Chris Evert in the final. She was ranked sixth in the world at the end of that year and won her first Grand Slam singles title in 1990, against the woman who would become her greatest rival, German star Steffi Graf.

Monica Seles, pictured in 1991.

At 16 and a half years of age, Seles won in straight sets, becoming the youngest ever winner of the French title. She climbed to world number two by the end of that year and by March 1991 overtook Graf as the world's number one player. Between 1991 and 1993, she dominated the game, reaching the final of 33 of the 34 tournaments in which she competed, and winning 22. At one stage her win-loss ratio stood at 92.9 percent – well ahead of the best male players of her era.

THE SCANDAL

Seles was playing in a match in the Citizen's Cup against Magdalena Maleeva of Bulgaria in Hamburg, Germany in April 1993. As she sat courtside with her back to the grandstand in a break between games, a man in the crowd lunged at her with a boning knife. The knife struck a shocked Seles once between the shoulder blades. With blood pouring from the wound, Seles staggered onto the court, screaming. She collapsed and the 6,000-strong crowd was in shock as security officers pounced on her assailant.

Seles was placed on a stretcher and rushed to hospital. Initial fears were that the attack was politically motivated because of Seles' Serbian heritage; she had been the subject of hate mail and death threats over the ongoing turmoil in Yugoslavia more than once. After interviewing the suspect, however, police were able to rule this out, announcing that Gunther Parche, 39, unemployed, had stabbed Seles because he was obsessed with Graf and wanted her to regain her ranking as the world's top player.

Doctors found the knife had penetrated around one and a half inches into Seles' upper back, missing vital organs. Seles stayed two days in hospital, suffering as much from shock as from her physical wounds, before being released. She avoided the public spotlight and became a victim of depression. "I felt empty and damaged inside," she explained later in her autobiography. "All I wanted to do was stuff myself with empty and damaging food."

THE AFTERMATH

The police described Parche as "mentally unstable". Six months after the stabbing, he appeared in court, only to be given a two-year suspended sentence by the trial judge, Elke Bosse. She said in view of Parche's psychological condition and expressions of extreme remorse, a jail term was not necessary. The verdict stunned Seles, who vowed never to play in Germany again. "What kind of message does this send to the world?" she asked.

Struggling to cope with the trauma, she checked into a clinic in the US state of Colorado. Her physical wounds healed quickly, but it took more than two years before she felt able to play competitive tennis again. She finally made her return in August 1995, winning her comeback tournament. The next month, she reached the US Open final, but lost … to Graf. She won the Australian Open early in 1996, among other successes, but was never the same dominant force she had been before the stabbing.

She retired from tennis after bowing out of the French Open in the first round, hampered by injury, in 2003. Six years later, she was elected into the International Tennis Hall of Fame and in 2011 she was named among the '30 Legends of Women's Tennis: Past, Present and Future' by TIME magazine. In recent years, she has been working as a Goodwill Ambassador for IIMSAM, an organisation committed to ending malnutrition in third-world countries.

THE SHERGAR KIDNAP MYSTERY, 1983

THE BACKGROUND

A speedy bay colt with a lightning turn of speed, Shergar was the pride of Irish horseracing. Foaled in 1978, he won the 1981 Epsom Derby by 10 lengths, the longest victory in the race's 200 year history. That win was rated amongst the 100 most memorable sporting moments of the twentieth century by Britain's influential *Observer* newspaper.

A handsome horse with a distinctive white blaze, Shergar was a popular performer, who revelled in being on the big stage. When he won the Irish Derby by four lengths, with famed jocky Lester Piggott on board, he became a national hero. Later that same year, he was named European Horse of the Year. His only loss as a three-year-old was a shock defeat in the St Leger Stakes at Doncaster.

It was then that Prince Aga Khan IV, Shergar's owner and one of the wealthiest men in the world at the time, decided to retire the horse to stud. The horse had a stud value of more than £10 million, and the Aga Khan sold 34 shares in the stallion at £250,000 each, retaining six shares himself. Shergar produced 35 foals in his only season at stud, the pick of the bunch being Authaal, who went on to win the 1986 Irish St Leger.

THE SCANDAL

In early February 1983, a car towing a horsebox drove into the Ballymany Stud Farm where Shergar was housed. Several armed men wearing hoods forced their way into the home of the horse's groom, James Fitzgerald. They held his family at gunpoint while ordering Fitzgerald to help load Shergar onto their horsebox. The horse was towed away while the thieves also kidnapped Fitzgerald, taking him in another car. After three hours, Fitzgerald was released, but there was no sign of Shergar.

The daring kidnapping made front-page news throughout Britain and a massive police investigation swung into action. But the thieves were clever – they had kidnapped Shergar on the day of Ireland's biggest horse sales, so there were thousands of horseboxes driving up and down roads throughout the country.

The thieves contacted the Aga Khan's representatives, asking for a massive ransom of around £5 million. They sent the police a photo of the horse's head next to a newspaper, as proof Shergar was still alive. But they failed to realise the prince was not Shergar's sole owner and the syndicate quickly decided against paying any ransom, believing it would make every good horse in the country fair game for similar kidnappings.

After four days, the kidnappers made their last call and were never heard from again. The syndicate blamed the Irish Republican Army (the IRA) for the crime, a theory that has gained momentum over the years.

THE AFTERMATH

Shergar's body was never found and no one was ever arrested. Making the police investigation tougher was a host of hoax calls and false sightings reported to both the authorities and to the media. There were many wild theories – one that he was kidnapped by Libya's Colonel Gaddafi, another that he was still alive and secretly producing foals. The IRA has never claimed responsibility for the crime but it is believed they were the most likely culprits, their motive being to use the ransom to buy arms.

The likely scenario, never substantiated, is that the kidnappers, having no experience in handling animals, would have had trouble controlling Shergar. Realising they would not get their ransom money, they may at first have decided to set Shergar free, but then, with the whole country on the lookout for the missing horse, decided it was too risky, fearing they would get caught. Despite widespread searches over the years, Shergar's body has never been found. Many owners lost the money they had invested in the horse; only those who had insured Shergar for theft or death were compensated.

The Shergar Cup was founded in 1999 in a mark of respect to the great stallion and is one of the most prestigious races on the British calendar. Held at Ascot, it is a battle between the best horses and riders in the word. Hollywood was also entranced by the tragic tale, producing a movie starring Mickey Rourke, *Shergar*, in 1999.

GROBBELAAR'S 'MR FIXIT' CHARGES, 1994

THE BACKGROUND

Born in South Africa in 1957, Bruce Grobbelaar had a tough ride to the top. A talented sportsman, he found himself fighting in the Rhodesian Army against Robert Mugabe's guerillas in a gritty bush war in the 1970s. "It was a struggle to survive," he said, years later. But survive Grobbelaar did, knocking back a scholarship opportunity with Major League Baseball to concentrate on his first love, soccer.

After starting his career with Highlanders FC in the city of Bulawayo, he moved to Durban City. After his national service, he was scouted by the Vancouver Whitecaps in Canada, playing one season there before joining British team Crewe Alexandra. From there he joined Liverpool as back-up keeper to Ray Clemence in 1981.

When Clemence moved to Tottenham that same season, Grobbelaar got his chance. He started out shakily, making unforced errors in his first season that tested the patience of his team and the fans. But Grobbelaar had ability and when he found form and confidence, he quickly won over the Liverpool faithful.

He played for the Reds for over 13 years, becoming a favourite with his flamboyant and often unorthodox style. In a famous incident in the European Cup final against A.S. Roma in 1984, he wobbled his legs to mock Roma's Francesco Graziani as he lined up a kick in the penalty shootout. Graziani missed the kick, and Grobbelaar became a legend as Liverpool won the final.

THE SCANDAL

English tabloid newspaper *The Sun* dropped a bombshell in 1994, accusing Grobbelaar of match-fixing. Using a secret video camera, the paper alleged they had recorded Grobbelaar talking to men, whom he thought represented a betting syndicate, about 'throwing' games for cash.

Police charged Grobbelaar with conspiracy to corrupt, along with two other players, Aston Villa striker John Fashanu and Wimbledon goalie Hans Segers. A Malaysian businessman, Heng Suan Lim, was also charged, but all three were later cleared. Grobbelaar's alleged business partner had approached *The Sun*, who arranged for the hotel room to be bugged, and recorded match-fixing plans apparently being discussed. Grobbelaar appeared to have been taped admitting bribes for various games, including one of £40,000 in a match against Newcastle.

Grobbelaar continually protested his innocence, claiming he was aware of the match-fixing sting, but had simply been playing along so that he could gather evidence and take it to the police to catch the crooks. Two lengthy and costly trials followed, in which the jury could not agree on a verdict, and the four were cleared late in 1997.

Grobbelaar subsequently sued *The Sun* for damages and won the sum of £85,000. The newspaper appealed the verdict, and it was overturned. A furious Grobbelaar took the case as high as Britain's House of Lords. There it was found that, while the actual allegations of match-fixing were not proved, there was ample evidence of dishonesty by the players. Grobbelaar's award was slashed to £1, the lowest amount possible under English law. To add to his pain, he was also ordered to pay *The Sun's* legal costs – around £500,000.

In handing down the judgement, Lord Bingham declared, "The tort of defamation protects those whose reputations have been unlawfully injured. It affords little or no protection to those who have, or deserve to have, no reputation deserving of legal protection . . . [Grobbelaar] had in fact acted in a way in which no decent or honest footballer would act and in a way which could, if not exposed and stamped on, undermine the integrity of a game which earns the loyalty and support of millions."

THE AFTERMATH

Grobbelaar was stunned by the verdict and unable to pay the costs, which left him feeling bitter about the English legal system. "You win in the court of law and yet they decide you have to pay the opposition," he said years later.

He was declared bankrupt, but continued to play for a series of clubs. In all, he played 573 top-class games, 440 of them for Liverpool, where he remains a favourite son. He won three FA Cups with the Reds, as well as six league titles.

After retirement, he moved back to his homeland of South Africa, where he took up coaching with mixed success. He hopes to return to Liverpool one day, as manager.

MASSACRE AT MUNICH, 1972

THE BACKGROUND

The world has never seen an uglier example of terrorism in sport than the incident now known as the Munich Massacre. Hosting the Olympics for the first time since the dark days of Nazi Germany in 1936, West Germany went out of its way to portray the Games as a friendly, open

The apartment complex where the athletes were held hostage.

event in the summer of 1972. Security was deliberately extremely low-key, a fact that alarmed the team from Israel from the moment they arrived in West Germany in preparation for the Games. The Middle East was an extremely volatile place in the early 1970s, with a radical terrorist group, Black September, carrying out devastating raids and hijackings that often resulted in a high death toll.

THE SCANDAL

In the early hours of 5 September, eight Black September terrorists, wearing black tracksuits and armed with pistols, hand grenades and assault rifles, jumped a fence and entered the Olympic village. The terrorists, believed to have been assisted in their endeavours by German neo-Nazis, headed straight for the Israeli athletes' apartments, armed with stolen keys.

Wrestling referee Yossef Gutfreund was woken by the commotion and yelled a warning that alerted athletes to the danger. But by then it was too late – the terrorists were in and several people were captured. Wrestling coach Moshe Weinberg resisted the intruders and was shot dead. Weightlifter Yossef Romano, an Israeli army veteran, also fought the terrorists and was killed. Nine hostages were captured in all. They were bound and gagged and the bloodied corpse of Romano was dumped at their feet as a warning against further resistance. The world watched in horror as images of the masked terrorists, holding loaded weapons on the balconies of the village, were shown around the globe. They made a series of demands, including the release of over 200 Palestinians jailed in Israel. To show they were serious, they threw Weinberg's dead body out the door of the Israeli apartments.

Officials demanded proof the hostages were still alive and were ushered into the apartment, where they saw the remaining hostages held at gunpoint, as negotiations began. The terrorists demanded a plane and were taken by bus, with their hostages, to a military airfield to board helicopters. German authorities set up an ambush at the airport with a team of snipers. The terrorists' leader, Luttif Atif, was shot in the thigh and wounded. A gun battle erupted and two of the terrorists were killed. One, believed to be Atif, then shot at the hostages, who were seated in a helicopter, from point blank range, before dropping a hand grenade in the carriage. All nine hostages died, as did six terrorists, as the police opened fire. Three terrorists were captured.

THE AFTERMATH

Officials suspended competition for the first time in the history of the modern Olympics as a shocked world struggled to come to grips with the tragedy. Over 80,000 spectators and athletes attended a memorial service, at which IOC President Avery Brundage angered many in the crowd by barely referring to the slain Israeli athletes. Most nations' flags were flown at half-mast on the day, but 10 Arab nations refused to lower theirs. There were calls to cancel the remainder of the Games, which continued after the brief break. As one athlete said, 'If you hold a party and one of the guests is murdered, you don't continue the party.'

The remaining members of the Israeli delegation left the Games and returned home. German inquiries into the massacre showed that security had been far too lax, and the response to the hostage situation totally inadequate. Meanwhile, the bodies of the dead Palestinian gunmen were flown to Libya, where they received heroes' funerals. The Israeli military response to the attack was quick – they bombed 10 known Palestine Liberation Organisation (PLO) bases in the Middle East, killing an estimated 200 people. The Israeli secret service, Mossad, also dispatched teams of agents to several locations worldwide to hunt down and kill all those responsible for the planning and execution of the raid. It is believed that all of the assassins but one have been executed by Mossad. This man remains in hiding somewhere in the Middle East. Memorials to the 11 Israeli athletes and officials who lost their lives were established in both Munich and Israel.

In 2012, German magazine *Der Spiegel* alleged West German authorities had covered up many aspects of the massacre and refused to accept any blame for the entire affair. The magazine also claimed German officials had been tipped off about the raid weeks beforehand, but refused to take any action.

SUFFRAGETTE'S FATAL SACRIFICE, 1913

THE BACKGROUND

Emily Davison was one of England's leading women's rights advocates at the turn of the 20th century. A radical suffragette, she fought against the British male establishment and found herself thrown behind bars more than once for her rebellious ways.

Devoted suffragette Emily Davison.

Davison was born in London in 1872, and studied literature at Royal Holloway College after winning a bursary at 19. But when her father died, her mother couldn't afford the fees and Davison dropped out, working as a governess. She also became a schoolteacher and used her wage to study at St Hugh's College in Oxford. She achieved first-class honours in her final exams, but women were not admitted to degrees at Oxford at the time.

In 1906, Davison joined a female

rights movement, the Women's Social and Political Union (WSPU). The movement was founded three years earlier by noted feminist Emily Pankhurst, uniting women who believed radical measures were needed to help achieve equal rights in a chauvinistic, conservative Britain. Before long, Davison quit teaching to join the movement on a fulltime basis. She quickly became a thorn in the side of the police and government, spending nine stints in jail of varying lengths. Her offences included arson, throwing stones and assault. During one of the jail terms, she went on a hunger strike; on another she attempted suicide by throwing herself down a staircase, believing the cause needed a martyr. She survived, but suffered major back injuries that were to cause her pain for the rest of her life.

THE SCANDAL

In June of 1913, Davison attended the biggest event on the British racing calendar, Epsom Day. While tens of thousands of people, including King George V and his wife and queen consort, Mary, flocked to Epsom to cheer on the horses, Davison had a very different purpose in mind.

As the horses rounded Tattenham Corner midway through the race, Davison stunned onlookers by slipping under the fence and right into the middle of the race. Holding a WSPU flag, she was narrowly missed by a couple of horses before being trampled by the King's horse, Anmer. The horrific accident, captured on film and nowadays readily found online, shows Davison bowled over by the speeding horse, falling to the ground unconscious.

The horse was felled by the impact, but uninjured, while jockey Herbert Jones was thrown a distance after impact. Along with Davison, he was taken to hospital, suffering from concussion. The King, most concerned by the incident, hurried down to the course, where he checked on the condition of Jones and the horse.

The Queen made a personal inquiry regarding Davison's injuries the following day, sending a messenger to the hospital. Davison suffered major head and chest injuries from the impact and never regained consciousness. She died in hospital four days later from a fractured skull.

THE AFTERMATH

Legend has it that Davison had decided to commit suicide to give the suffragettes their martyr, but this is the subject of some debate. A return train ticket to London and a ticket to a dance that night were found in her pockets, while she also had a visit to her sister in France planned the following week. Supporters claim she was merely intending to stand in the middle of the track holding the WSPU flag to draw attention to the cause, while others claim there is no way she could have deliberately targeted the King's horse. She entered the course from a blind corner, with no live commentary of the race to to allow her to identify the horses, which came upon her at breakneck speed. There were also reports at the time that in the weeks leading up to the race, she practised grabbing horses while they were galloping near her mother's house in the suburb of Morpeth.

Jones recovered from the fall but was haunted by the accident for the remainder of his life. When Pankhurst died in 1928, he laid a wreath at the funeral as a tribute to both her and Davison. He died in 1951 in his kitchen, which had been filled with gas. In 1999, English Labour MP Tony Benn revealed he had erected a small plaque with a photo of Emily Davison in his cupboard at the House of Commons. The plaque commemorated another of Davison's daring deeds, when she hid in the Palace of Westminster during the 1911 national census. When the census asked for her address that day, Davison correctly declared "The House of Commons".

Benn explained: "It is a modest reminder of a great woman with a great cause, who never lived to see it prosper, but played a significant part in making it possible."

ITALIAN MARATHON HERO DISQUALIFIED, 1908

THE BACKGROUND

Over 100,000 people crammed into London's White City Stadium during the 1908 Olympics to watch what promised to be one of the Games' highlights – the marathon. The race was due to start outside Windsor Castle, but Princess Mary (great-grandmother to Queen Elizabeth II), wanted her children to see the beginning of the race, so it was moved back 200 yards inside the castle grounds, to a spot near the nursery. The marathon distance then became 26 miles, 385 yards, which it has been ever since . . . and though no one knew it at the time, those extra 200 yards would prove very crucial.

Dorando Pietri approaching the marthon finish line.

There were a host of fancied runners in the 55-man field, but Italian Dorando Pietri was not one of them. A sweet shop employee in his hometown of Capri, Pietri stood just 1.59 metres, or 5ft 2½in, tall, and looked considerably younger than his 23 years. Several English runners had strong claims to the gold medal and Queen Alexandra herself sent a telegram to the princess to signal the start of the race.

The runners took off at 2.30pm on a hot London afternoon and as the crowd waited in the stadium, they watched other events including 'catch-as-catch-can', wrestling and diving. Every few minutes, the name of the leader of the race was read out to the crowd as the tension mounted.

THE SCANDAL

After nearly three hours, the diminutive figure of Pietri staggered into the stadium. Suffering from cramps and dehydration, Pietri was well clear of the field but fading fast. With the finish line just a couple of hundred yards away, Pietri staggered and collapsed in a heap. The crowd gasped, with the clerk of the course, Jack Andrew, and medical officer Dr Michael Bulger running to his aid. They helped a disorientated Pietri to his feet, and in doing so ensured the popular Italian would be disqualified. In his memoirs, written years later, Andrew explained, "As Dorando reached the track he staggered and after a few yards fell. I kept would-be helpers at bay, but Dr Bulger went to his assistance. I warned him that this would entail disqualification, but he replied that although I was in charge of the race, I must obey him. Each time Dorando fell I had to hold his legs while the doctor massaged him to keep his heart beating."

Famed writer Sir Arthur Conan Doyle was among the masses cheering Pietri on. "It is horrible, and yet fascinating, this struggle between a set purpose and an utterly exhausted frame," Doyle commented. "Amid stooping figures and grasping hands I caught a glimpse of the haggard, yellow face, the glazed, expressionless eyes, the long, black hair streaked across the bow. Surely he is done now."

A second runner, American Johnny Hayes, suddenly entered the arena. With the pro-British crowd desperate for an American not to claim gold, several other 'helpers' arrived, virtually carrying an exhausted Pietri over the finish line to the cheers of the capacity crowd.

THE AFTERMATH

Hayes finished the race without any such problems in second place and promptly lodged a protest against Pietri. The distraught Pietri was disqualified, a move that a newspaper of the day described as "draconian and pitiless". But Queen Alexandra took pity on the luckless Italian and arranged for him to be presented with a special silver cup at the Games' closing ceremony.

Then, through his newspaper, the *Daily Mail*, Doyle started an appeal to enable Pietri to open a bakery in his hometown. Doyle kicked off the fund with £5, and the drive generated £300 – a considerable sum in that day.

Because of the circumstances of his loss, Pietri became an instant celebrity. Two months after the Olympics, he went by boat to New York, where a rematch was staged against Hayes at Madison Square Garden. A full house of 20,000 watched the two athletes run 262 laps around the arena, with Pietri winning by half a lap. Pietri continued to run exhibition events throughout the USA to massive crowds, winning 17 of his 22 races. Famed composer Irving Berlin wrote a song about him and Pietri continued to run until retiring in 1911, appropriately winning his final race, in his homeland of Italy. Pietri used his winnings to open a hotel with his brother, but it went bust. He died aged 56 in his hometown of Capri. On the 100th anniversary of his Olympic triumph and tragedy, the locals unveiled a huge statue of Pietri, captioned simply "Pietri the Winner".

BLACK SUNDAY, 1920

THE BACKGROUND

The Irish War of Independence from 1919 to 1921 was a bloody guerilla war between the Irish Republican Army and the British government's forces in Ireland. The British formed a paramilitary force known as the Black and Tans and both sides used brutal and violent tactics toward both each other and civilians. IRA Intelligence chief Michael Collins planned to eliminate a group of British officers and spies, and on the morning of Sunday 21 November 1920, teams began sweeping through Dublin.

There were 50 names on Collins' original hit list, but it was whittled down to 35 by other IRA officials, who claimed there was insufficient evidence against the rest. Within hours, 13 people were dead and six more injured, with skirmishes erupting throughout the city. While many of the attacks were bungled, Collins did succeed in sending a wave of panic throughout the British ranks in the country.

Collins explained his actions later: "My one intention was the destruction of the undesirables who continued to make miserable the lives of ordinary decent citizens. I have proof enough to assure myself of the atrocities which this gang of spies and informers have committed . . . By their destruction the very air is made sweeter. For myself, my conscience is clear. There is no crime in detecting in wartime the spy and the informer. They have been destroyed without trial. I have paid them back in their own coin."

THE SCANDAL

The same afternoon, the Dublin Gaelic football team was set to play Tipperary at Croke Park, the major ground of the Gaelic Athletic Association. Despite news spreading like wildfire of unrest in the city due to Collins' raids, over 5,000 fans flocked to Croke Park to witness the game. But, unknown to the fans, hundreds of British troops were milling nearby and had orders to raid the game.

Two groups, one from the northwest and one from the south, moved in, as fans took their seats for the 3.15pm kickoff. The troops had orders to surround the arena, block the exits and search every man in the park. They reached the stadium 10 minutes after the game began and when the masses saw them, pandemonium ensued. Shots began to ring out, with both the British and the IRA claiming the other side fired first. The British believed the ticket sellers at the gates were actually IRA sentries and began trying to round them up. The ticket sellers ran, and troops began to open fire. That triggered panic within the stands, as spectators ran for the exits, fearing for their lives. The gunfire lasted an estimated 90 seconds. Over 100 rifle shots had been fired by the time order was restored, as well as untold numbers of pistol shots. When the dust settled, seven people were dead, five more were critical and two had been trampled to death in the melee. Two of the players were shot – Michael Hogan died, while Jim Egan was among the many wounded.

After order had been restored, security forces completed their mission, searching all the men at the arena. They found just one pistol.

THE AFTERMATH

As the raid had not been officially sanctioned, the Crown went into damage control, releasing a press statement saying many of the gunmen from earlier in the day had been hiding in the crowd. It went on to say that the plan was for an officer to address the crowd, inviting the assassins to come forward, but that they then panicked and started the disorder. This was ridiculed by those who witnessed the events on the day. Eyewitnesses told a later inquiry that the troops fired on the crowd without any provocation. The commander of the raid, Major Mills, later told an inquiry that his men were "excited and out of hand".

A military court ruled that "the fire on the RIC [Royal Irish Constabulary] was carried out without orders and exceeded the demands of the situation". The findings of the court were kept secret by the British Government and were only fully revealed 80 years later. The events of Black Sunday, as it became known, turned the public against the Crown. Even the King was said to be horrified by the actions of the day. A ceasefire was finally declared in July 1921, with a treaty ending the British rule of Ireland six months later. As a tribute to Michael Hogan, the Gaelic Athletic Association named one of the grandstands at Croke Park 'The Hogan Stand'. He was just 24 when he died.

OLYMPIC PIN-UP GIRL TURNS ESCORT, 2012

THE BACKGROUND

Suzy Favor Hamilton has been one of the USA's best middle distance runners of the modern generation. A graduate of the University of Wisconsin, with the most NCAA titles in history, she competed at three Olympic Games. But unlike many US stars, who won fame and fortune, Favor Hamilton missed out on the gold rush. In fact, she has no medals to show for her long Olympic career and gave an insight into the pressure "average" athletes find themselves under, in an incident at the Sydney 2000 Games. The gold medal favourite in the 1500 metres, after having posted the world's fastest time just three months earlier, Favor Hamilton felt the heavy weight of expectation in Sydney. She was well placed before entering the final stages of the race, when two runners passed her.

Seeing her Olympic gold medal dream crumble, Favor Hamilton made a remarkable decision – to fall to the ground. "These two girls took my dream and my life away," she explained. "That moment, I remember thinking, 'I can't not win this race – this is not how I planned this.' When my head hit the ground it was like a light turned on and I remember saying to myself, 'You're an idiot. You just fell in the Olympic finals, get up. You are a loser if you don't finish the race.'

"That was probably the first time I told myself I was a loser. So I got up and got over the finish line . . . I felt like I let everybody down and it completely destroyed me."

That was Favor Hamilton's final Olympic moment. She trained for the 2004 Olympics but pulled out shortly before the Games. In 2005 she announced she was suffering from depression and had contemplated suicide. Her career was over but in 2012 she made the kind of worldwide headlines that had eluded her during her running career.

THE SCANDAL

A tabloid website, The Smoking Gun, broke a story in December 2012 that Favor Hamilton, who was married and had a young daughter, was sponsored by Nike, and did promotional work for Disney, was working as a $600-an-hour call girl in Las Vegas. The website claimed Favor Hamilton worked for an escort service, Haley Heston's Private Collection, and while she called herself Kelly, she told several of her clients her true identity.

The athlete eventually acknowledged that the story was true. "I take full responsibility for my mistakes," she told the website. "I'm not the victim and I'm not going down that route. I'm owning up to what I did. I would not blame anybody except myself."

She added, "Everybody in this world makes mistakes. I made a huge mistake. Huge."

At the time, Favor Hamilton operated a successful real estate brokerage in Wisconsin with her husband and also delivered motivational speeches and did promotional work. She told the website that her husband Mark knew of her 'other' life. "He tried, he tried to get me to stop," she said. "He wasn't supportive of this at all."

The former Olympian believed she was 'outed' by one of the clients to whom she revealed her identity. "He totally broke all the rules by outing me," she said. "I don't want to be like him. Because he is scum. And I will not become scum to make myself feel good. I will not do it. I would suffer rather than go that route of being vindictive."

THE AFTERMATH

Afterwards, Favor Hamilton blamed her ongoing battle with depression. "I do not expect people to understand," Favor Hamilton posted on Twitter. "But the reasons for doing this made sense to me at the time and were very much related to depression."

She added she was "not a victim here and knew what I was doing. I was drawn to escorting in large part because it provided many coping mechanisms for me when I was going through a very challenging time with my marriage and my life."

The sporting public was stunned by the revelations, particularly when it was further revealed that the Favor Hamiltons – husband, wife and young daughter – lived in a comfortable $600,000 home in Madison, Wisconsin, with no apparent financial problems. The Disney Corporation, one of Favor Hamilton's strongest supporters, disowned her after the scandal, declaring her banned from competing in any of their events; she had until then been a regular participant in the Disneyland Half-Marathon.

But the furore made Favor Hamilton realise the error of her ways. She tweeted at the end of it all, "I fully intend to make amends and get back to being a good mother, wife, daughter and friend."

UNIVERSITY FOOTBALL TEAM'S 'DEATH PENALTY', 1986

THE BACKGROUND

Southern Methodist University was one of the best-known teams in American college football for over 50 years. They were crowned national champions in 1935 and won 10 titles in the strong Southwest Conference, which included many of the best teams in Texas. After a lean period in the 1950s and 1960s, the Mustangs experienced a golden era in the early 1980s, losing just five of 51 games and winning three Southwest Conferences. The team moved its home field to Texas Stadium, home of the legendary Dallas Cowboys, and drew massive crowds, rivalling the NFL for popularity during Dallas' boomtown days.

SMU achieved all these remarkable feats despite being the second-smallest school in the Southwest Conference with an enrolment of less than 10,000 students. Nevertheless, it felt the pressure to match the bigger schools in the conference, like Texas A and M, and Oklahoma, and was sanctioned for recruiting violations several times. Schools were not allowed to pay players to entice them to the college, but the practice was commonplace – at one stage, five of the nine members of the Southwest Conference were under some form of probation for bending or breaking the rules. But SMU was under the microscope more than their rivals, because they were caught more than any other school. From 1974 to 1985, they were sanctioned seven times. Boosters who were intent on seeing the school return to its former glory put large amounts of money towards attracting talent, and administrators often turned a blind eye.

THE SCANDAL

The first major blow came when offensive lineman Sean Stopperich, who joined SMU from Pennsylvania, told NCAA investigators that he had received several thousand dollars to renege on a deal with the University of Pittsburgh to join the Mustangs. SMU was banned from Bowl games for 1985 and 1986 as a result, and were also barred from appearing on live television.

Then in 1986, a Dallas TV station, WFAA-TV, broke a story that another player, David Stanley, claimed SMU paid him $25,000 to sign on in 1983 and had continued to pay him monthly, even after the college had been punished over the Stopperich incident. It was also revealed that tight end Albert Reese had allegedly been living in an apartment in Dallas rent-free, with a well-known SMU booster allegedly handling the bills. These latest transgressions came just months after the NCAA held a crisis meeting in New Orleans in which schools voted to consider suspending the football program of any team found to have broken the rules twice in the space of five years.

The NCAA stunned the nation by invoking what was known as the 'death penalty', banishing SMU from playing any football for the entire 1987 season. It invoked the harshest penalty in US sports history to "eliminate a program that was built on a legacy of wrongdoing, deceit and rule violations". The NCAA slammed SMU, declaring its football program was "built on a legacy of wrongdoing, deceit and rule violations".

THE AFTERMATH

The decision created massive tension in Dallas, which prided itself on SMU's record. *The Dallas Times Herald*, which broke several stories related to the scandal, lost advertising revenue and circulation as a result. David Berst, chairman of the Infractions Committee that handed down the judgement, fainted in front of the cameras after making the announcement of the death penalty. Berst said the committee looked at lesser penalties, but given SMU's continual flouting of the rules, declared "there simply didn't seem to be any options left".

Players were all granted releases, with many quickly snapped up by rival schools. After losing their best players, SMU announced it would not field a team in 1988 either, because of lack of playing talent. The school fielded a team again in 1989 but, having lost the ability to give out 55 scholarships as a further part of their punishment, the team struggled to compete. In the two decades after the death penalty, the Mustangs had just one winning season. The Southwest Conference also suffered a massive dent to its reputation over the infractions by SMU and other schools, and was disbanded in 1996. In 2009, the Mustangs finally returned to a Bowl game, making the Hawaii Bowl, in which they beat Nevada.

Since 1987, over 30 schools have been caught violating rules twice within five years, yet only two small schools have received the death penalty – one for soccer and the other for tennis. Former University of Florida president John Lombardi explained, "SMU taught the committee that the death penalty is too much like the nuclear bomb … the results were so catastrophic that now we'll do anything to avoid dropping another one."

WOMAN DIES AFTER DRUGS WITH HERO, 2000

THE BACKGROUND

Gary Ablett's nickname, 'God', said it all – such was the esteem in which this former Australian Rules football legend was held. A superstar of the game to fans in the 1980s and 1990s, Ablett was among the most brilliant attacking players the game has ever seen, a remarkable goal-kicker with the ability to take spectacular marks.

Born in the country town of Druin in 1961, Ablett was signed by Hawthorn in 1982, but struggled to adapt to life in the big city. He went back to the country before returning to Melbourne with the Geelong club in 1984. He quickly established himself as an attacking force and went on to play nearly 250 games for the club, booting over 1,000 goals and playing in four grand finals. Ablett retired in 1991, citing a lack of hunger for the win and personal issues, before returning to football five months later. He was inducted into the AFL's Hall of Fame after retiring (again) in 1997 and was also named in the AFL Team of the Century. He won three Coleman Medals, four All-Australian jumpers and played for Victoria 11 times. He is the only player in the game's history to win three Coleman Medals and kick 100 goals in a season for three straight years.

THE SCANDAL

Ablett battled drug problems and depression during and after his career. He was placed on a good behaviour bond for assault in 1990, after an attack on a man he found with his estranged wife. He fell into what he later termed the "wrong crowd" late in his career, and his drug use spiralled.

Then in 2000, Ablett found himself at the centre of a storm when a 19-year-old woman,

Alisha Horan, died of a drug overdose in his Park Hyatt hotel room in Melbourne. Ablett initially declined to answer police questions about the death, which was found to be from a combination of heroin, ecstasy and amphetamines. Ablett eventually gave his version of events – that he brought the drugs to the hotel to use himself. "Basically she caught me with it," he said in a statement to police two years later. "She asked what it was. I didn't really want her knowing that it was what it was [drugs]. I told her it was cocaine and she wanted some."

Ablett and Horan, a fan, were already "wasted" from a long session of drinking. Ablett was drunk and tired, but alleged that he didn't want his young companion to use heroin. Ablett claimed to have given her access to only a tiny amount, and that he himself had "six or eight times" what he gave Ms Horan, but hours later she was dead from an overdose.

Ablett said he made the confession due to his religious beliefs and a heavy heart, which required him to "reveal the facts as they happened". He declined to give evidence at an inquiry into Ms Horan's death, but claimed it was because the young girl's family did not want him to give details of their liasion to protect her reputation.

In March 2001, coroner Noreen Toohey ruled that Ms Horan died from a deadly combination of heroin, ecstasy and amphetamines. She commented that Ms Horan had "become enmeshed in a culture of alcoholism and drug taking with her football hero" and was partying "out of her league". She criticised Ablett for failing to "protect their [the Horan family's] young daughter when she was in trouble".

THE AFTERMATH

Ablett was not charged over Ms Horan's death, but was fined $1,500 by police, for using and possessing heroin. Ablett expressed what appeared to be genuine remorse over the incident in 2007, because he did not want to profit from her death in an upcoming book. "It's a football book and I don't think it's appropriate and I don't want to be in any way profiting from that tragedy," he said. "Apart from the pain and grief of the tragedy, I feel a deep sense of shame and failure over my own behaviour and I still feel deep regret and remorse. I wish I had a time machine … I can't begin to imagine the pain suffered by those close to Alisha … After it happened I could not get out of bed for about six weeks, such was the devastation."

But his apology only served to further anger the Horan family. Alisha's father Alan said he never wanted to speak to the former star again, despite the apology. "I wouldn't want to," Horan said. "It's rubbish, crap, end of story."

GIANTS STEAL SIGNS VIA TELESCOPE, 1951

THE BACKGROUND

Stealing signs in baseball has always been a grey area. The communication between catcher and pitcher via a system of complicated hand signals is as old as the game itself, and more than once rival teams have attempted to intercept these supposedly secret messages. Major League Baseball formally outlawed sign stealing by mechanical devices in the 1960s, but when the New York Giants won the World Series in 1951, regarded as one of the most remarkable feats in baseball history, signs were still more or less fair game. But recently, after more than 50 years of silence and innuendo, journalists have uncovered amazing details of a scheme developed by then Giants manager Leo Durocher to steal catchers' signs via a telescope hidden in the team's clubhouse and relayed by an electronic buzzer system.

Giants manager Leo Durocher, pictured here in 1948.

Midway through that famous season of 1951, the Giants were struggling. In August,

they were 13½ games behind the Dodgers and playing poorly. But suddenly they put on a late surge that won them a place in the game's folklore, winning 16 straight games. Significantly, 13 of these 16 games were at home, where Durocher had his controversial sign-stealing system in place.

THE SCANDAL

Desperate for an edge, Durocher positioned one of his staff, former catcher Herman Franks, with a powerful telescope in the Giants' clubhouse, trained on the opposition catcher.

Before taking this radical step, Durocher consulted his players. Some wanted the signs, others did not. "It was about 50/50," recalled pitcher Al Corwin. But Durocher went ahead, setting Franks up and arming him with an electronic buzzer that relayed signals to the Giants' bullpen. A reserve catcher, Sal Yvars, listened for the buzzer. One buzz meant a fast ball, two buzzes meant a slower delivery. Yvars then tossed a ball in the air for a curveball, and sat motionless for a fast ball. The batter could glance over the pitcher's shoulder to the bullpen to get the signs. It gave the Giants an immediate edge. "Every hitter knew what was coming," former pitcher Al Gettel admitted years later. "It made a big difference."

The Dodgers had their suspicions their signs were being stolen, with their captain, Charlie Dressen, smelling a rat. At one stage, he even took a pair of binoculars into the dugout to take a close look around the arena. "The umpire spotted us," Dodgers coach Cookie Lavagetto said later. "He ran over and grabbed the binoculars away from us. There was nothing we could do."

In the National League pennant-deciding game, the Giants trailed the Brooklyn Dodgers 4-2 in the bottom of the ninth when Bobby Thompson walked to the plate. With two men on base, Thompson famously hit a pitch from Ralph Branca for a home run, winning the game for the Giants in what has become known in sports history as 'The Shot Heard Round The World'.

THE AFTERMATH

The recently unearthed evidence of sign stealing has created a controversy – did Thompson use the ploy to win the decider? "Stealing signs is nothing to be proud of," Thompson said in an interview many, many years later. "Of course, the question is, did I take the sign that day?" Thompson hit more than .100 higher than before the Giants began sign stealing, but had always insisted, since the scandal became public knowledge in 2001, that he did not. "My answer is no," he said when prodded. "I was always proud of that swing."

Sign stealing aside, Thompson's effort remains a magical piece of sporting theatre. *The Sporting News* named it the greatest moment in baseball history, while *Sports Illustrated* ranked it the second-greatest sports moment of the 20th century (after the US team's ice hockey win over Russia at the 1980 Olympics at Lake Placid). A nation mourned when Thompson died in 2010, aged 87.

Durocher had a long and successful career as a manager, winning 2,008 games. He died in 1991. Branca suffered a back injury the following year, 1952, and won just 12 more games before retiring. He has always refused to buy into the controversy, stating gracefully, "I didn't want to look like I was crying over spilled milk. Bobby and I were really, really good friends. He still hit the pitch."

'CHUCKER' PRESSURED OUT OF CRICKET, 1963

THE BACKGROUND

The gentlemanly game of cricket found itself embroiled in a controversy regarding bowling actions in the 1950s and 1960s. Several bowlers found themselves under the microscope of officials, who were under pressure to stamp out bowlers who used a "chucking" action with a bent arm rather than a bowling action. And none was in the cross-hairs more than Australian fast bowler Ian Meckiff.

Born in Victoria in 1935, Meckiff won a place in cricket history in 1960 when he was run out by West Indian Joe Solomon in 1960, resulting in the first tied Test the game had ever seen. Meckiff had an unconventional, front-on bowling style that started to raise eyebrows among officials on the lookout for illegal actions. Against England in 1958–59, he achieved good results, taking nine wickets to lead Australia to victory at the Melbourne Cricket Ground in the second Test. After the game, several English journalists accused Meckiff of a "throwing" action. The controversy became front-page news in the English tabloids, pushing the Cold War inside the newspapers. Australian critics hit back, claiming if Meckiff was a thrower, then so were several English bowlers. The rules at the time stated: "For a delivery to be fair, the ball must be bowled, not thrown or jerked; if either umpire be not entirely satisfied of the absolute fairness of a delivery in this respect, he shall call and signal no-ball instantly upon delivery."

The English did not formally complain about Meckiff's actions, although it was later revealed captain Peter May was considering doing so, but did not want to be branded a sore loser.

THE SCANDAL

In 1960, international cricket officials changed the rules to ban straightening the arm at the point of the ball's delivery. But the change angered Australia, with cricket boss Bill Dowling accusing the English media and establishment of pre-judging Meckiff by intimidating umpires through the media.

In 1962–63, the Australian Cricket Board told umpires to toughen up on enforcing the rules, particularly in relation to throwing. The pressure also mounted in England, with the *News of the World* saying "there is no room in cricket for throwers. Let us hope that . . . the Australian selectors realise this . . . otherwise the throwing war will be waged in earnest."

Meckiff was chosen for Australia for the first Test against South Africa, prompting speculation as to whether umpires Lou Rowan and Col Egar would rule his action illegal. Meckiff bowled his first over, in which four deliveries were ruled no-balls by umpire Egar. This created a furore, with the crowd heckling the umpire and demanding a fair go for Meckiff. Egar insisted he had not bowed to pressure to ban Meckiff. "My only judgement was what I saw at the time," he said later. Ironically, Meckiff and Egar were close friends, having played lawn bowls together only weeks before the incident.

The over finally ended, and Meckiff didn't bowl again in the match. He retired at the end of the game and never played top-class cricket again, although he insisted his action was still legitimate, having been declared fair for virtually his entire time in the game.

THE AFTERMATH

At the end of play, fans invaded the field and carried the shattered bowler from the field on their shoulders. Police had to escort the umpires from the ground, with Egar receiving death threats over the incident. Egar met with Meckiff in the Australian dressing room at the end of the day's play, with the two exchanging words and a brief hug. Egar later said he was "the second-most upset person in the world".

The entire affair remains one of the most unsavoury in Australia's long sporting history, with many convinced that Meckiff, a popular man and all-round good guy, had been deliberately chosen by selectors so he would be no-balled. Meckiff's drumming out of the game became a bitter issue, with Australian manager Barry Gibbs labelling the "humiliation" of Meckiff as "without a doubt the most dramatic and emotion-charged" sporting moment he had ever seen. Sydney's *Daily Mirror* called the luckless Meckiff "the most obvious fall-guy in Australian cricket history". Reports say the crowd was close to rioting, with play halted at one stage as fans chanted the bowler's name and abused the umpires.

Meckiff retained a dignifed stance in retirement, but did say the no-ball calls that ended his career were "like a dagger in the back". He described umpire Egar as "a fair and just man who acted according to his convictions".

GOLD MEDAL WINNER'S GENDER SECRET, 1980

THE BACKGROUND

In 1980, the parking lot of a discount store in Cleveland, Ohio became the scene of a robbery gone wrong. The bandits attempted to mug an elderly woman and she fought back, trying to knock the gun from one of their hands. The weapon went off, the bullet lodging in her abdomen. Stella Walsh, aged 69, was rushed to a nearby hospital but died from her injuries several hours later.

When medical examiners performed an autopsy, they were stunned to learn that Walsh had male sexual organs. She actually possessed what were termed at the time as "ambiguous genitalia", which could not be easily identified as either male or female. Further examination allegedly found that she had both male and female chromosomes, as well as no female sex organs. But the mystery deepened when police inquiries revealed that Walsh was previously known as Stanislawa Walasiewicz – and that in 1932, she was the fastest woman in the world and Olympic gold medallist.

THE SCANDAL

Born in Poland in 1911, Stella Walsh, as she became known, moved to the US with her family while still a baby. In her teenage years, Walsh showed tremendous promise and won several national titles in sprinting. The city of Cleveland even awarded the promising athlete a car when she was in her late teens. The USA was keen to have Walsh represent them at the Olympics and she was offered American citizenship, but declined only days before the ceremony. This upset many Americans, as Walsh was a superstar at the time – she won three events at US national championship meets four times, a feat that has never been matched to this day.

Despite living in Cleveland and working there as a clerk, she represented Poland in the 1932 Los Angeles Olympics, winning gold in the prestige event of the Games, the 100-yard sprint, and equalling the world record of 11.9 seconds. It was no fluke; two years earlier, Walsh became the first woman to break the 11-second mark for 100 yards and, ironically, one press report of the time spoke of her 'man-like strides'. Walsh became an instant hero in Poland, returning to her country of birth after the Olympics to the acclaim of massive crowds. Four years later, in Berlin, Walsh was again one of the favourites for the 100-yard crown, but finished just behind 6-foot American farm girl Helen Stephens. Walsh and Stephens became bitter rivals and in a further touch of irony, irate Polish journalists accused Stephens of being a man. German officials were forced to issue a statement 24 hours after the race that Stephens had been given a sex check, and passed.

Walsh continued to run in the US, though never with the same success as in her two Olympic campaigns. With her native Poland overrun by the Nazis, and then the Russians, she remained in the USA and finally accepted citizenship in 1947. She married a boxer, Neil Olsen, but the marriage was brief. She won her last US national title in 1951 at the age of 40 and retired soon afterwards to a quiet life in Cleveland.

THE AFTERMATH

The truth about Walsh wasn't to come out until 44 years after her last Olympic showing, after that fateful car park shootout. There are some claims that Walsh was in fact a hermaphrodite – a person with both XX and XY chromosomes. There were moves to scrap her name from the record books, but they have since come to nought. At the time of her death, a coroner determined she had a mixture of male and female chromosomes. He added that Walsh had no internal female reproductive organs, and possessed a non-functioning penis, "masculine" breasts and an abnormal urinary opening.

Her case is said to be one of the major reasons the International Olympic Committee has dropped its gender-testing program. The issue flared up again in 2009, with the arrival on the scene of controversial South African runner Caster Semenya. After extensive testing and a worldwide controversy, Semanya was allowed to run as a woman in a landmark case in 2010.

Stella Walsh set over 100 records in her life and her time for the 100-yard sprint remains a European record, although races are not measured in yards anymore. A recreation building in Cleveland is named in her honour.

PETE ROSE BANNED, 1989

THE BACKGROUND

Pete Rose was a sensational baseball player whose career spanned three decades. Born in 1941, he attended high school in Ohio and was signed by the Cincinnati Reds straight after graduation. He made his Major League Baseball debut against Pittsburgh in 1963 and got his first hit five days later, against the Pirates. He found form and confidence quickly and was named National League Rookie of the Year after hitting .273 for the season. A switch hitter, Rose went on to become the all-time MLB leader in hits, games played (a mammoth 3,562), at bats and outs.

He won three World Series rings in a distinguished career at the Reds, Philadelphia Phillies and Montreal Expos. A tough competitor, dubbed "Charlie Hustle", he also won an MVP award, two Golden Gloves and played 17 All-Star games in an unprecedented five different positions. In 1975 he was named *Sports Illustrated* magazine's Sportsman of the Year and four years later became the highest paid athlete in team sports when he signed a $3.2 million deal with the Phillies. Returning home to Cincinnati as player-manager in 1984, he broke Ty Cobb's all-time hits record before retiring from playing, late in 1986.

THE SCANDAL

There were unconfirmed reports in the mid to late 1980s that Rose, then fulltime manager of the Reds, had a gambling problem. Rumours were rife that he had bet on baseball. He was questioned by the game's commissioner, Peter Ueberroth, but Rose steadfastly denied the allegations and the probe ended. When Ueberroth was succeeded by Bart Giamatti, a fresh investigation, chaired by high-profile lawyer John Dowd, was launched.

Sports Illustrated, who 14 years earlier had named Rose their man of the year, wrote a series of damning articles claiming the former star had bet heavily on baseball in March and April of 1989. After interviewing a series of bookies and intermediaries, Dowd handed his findings to Commissioner Giamatti in May. His investigation found that Rose had bet on games on a regular basis from 1985 to 1987. Dowd claimed Rose gambled a minimum of $10,000 per game, but there was no evidence he ever bet against his own team.

Rose angrily denied the allegations, refusing to front a hearing, and at one stage threatening legal action against Giamatti. He claimed Giamatti had prejudiced the case and that, as a result, he could not get a fair hearing. After much legal manoeuvring, Rose entered into settlement negotiations. In August 1989, Pete Rose voluntarily accepted a permanent place on MLB's ineligible list.

THE AFTERMATH

Rose came to a compromise with officialdom – he took the ban without admitting any wrongdoing and MLB, for its part, made no formal finding or charge of gambling against him. Rose ended his tenure as Reds manager, but planned to apply for reinstatement after a year.

Worse was to follow for the fallen star, with Rose spending five months in a medium security prison in Illinois in 1990, after pleading guilty to tax evasion. He was fined $50,000 and paid over $350,000 in back taxes. The following year, the Hall of Fame formally declared that it would refuse to induct former players who were on the permanently ineligible list. Despite this, Rose was selected as an outfielder in the MLB All-Century team, with a list of 100 players chosen by a panel of experts and then voted on by the public. As such, his ban was temporarily lifted. He was introduced to the crowd during the 1999 World Series in Atlanta to massive applause.

Rose applied for reinstatement in 1992 and 1997, failing both times. After years of denials, Rose finally admitted he had bet on baseball in his autobiography *My Prison Without Bars*, released in 2004. In a 2007 radio interview, he said, "I didn't bet on my team four nights of the week, I bet on my team to win every night, because I loved my team and I believed in my team. I did everything in my power every night to win that game."

Dowd disputes Rose's statement that he bet on his team every night, alleging that he did not bet on them at times when his star pitchers were absent. Rose's battle with the bookies and subsequent ban from the game became the subject of a 2004 ESPN TV movie, *Hustle*.

NFL'S VIDEO SPIES EXPOSED, 2006

THE BACKGROUND

The NFL has strict rules in place against teams videoing the signals used by rival coaches during matches. Most leading figures in the game believed there was no advantage to be gained from taping and then studying rival coaches anyway, but the NFL insisted the rule stay in place to prevent incidents of 'spying' by coaches on their opponents.

Rumours were rife over the years that some coaches and teams were flouting the rule, resulting in the NFL sending out a specific directive to clubs in early September 2006. It read, in part, "Videotaping of any type, including but not limited to taping of an opponent's offensive or defensive signals, is prohibited on the sidelines, in the coaches' booth, in the locker room or at any other locations accessible to club staff members during the game."

On 9 September, NFL security officials confiscated a video camera and tapes used by New England Patriots' video assistant Matt Estrella on the sidelines of a game in the opening round of the season against the New York Jets. The move came after a complaint by Jets coach Eric Mangini, a former Patriots assistant coach.

THE SCANDAL

Two days later, NFL commissioner Roger Goodell determined that the Patriots violated the league's rules by filming the Jets' defensive signals. Allegations began to surface that the Patriots had shot unauthorised video on previous occasions. Patriots coach Bill Belichick subsequently issued an apology, saying he "misinterpreted" the rule. He said that he believed if video shot during a game was not used during that actual game, its collection was legal.

The NFL still came down heavily on Belichick, fining him $500,000, the biggest fine ever imposed in the game's history. The Patriots were fined an additional $250,000 and had to forfeit their first-round pick in the following year's NFL draft. Furthermore, the Patriots were ordered to hand over all video, notes and other material related to the incident to the NFL. The Patriots complied and, after reviewing the material, the NFL destroyed it.

Former Dallas Cowboys coach Jimmy Johnson acknowledged Belichick did the wrong thing, but added he believed other coaches used similar tactics and went unpunished. Former Miami coach Don Shula commented that if the Patriots produced a perfect regular season, which they went on to do, the NFL should consider putting an asterisk next to their name.

THE AFTERMATH

Early in 2008, in a strongly worded letter that was made public, US Senator Arlen Specter wrote to NFL Commissioner Goodell, describing the destruction of the Patriots' tapes as "inexplicable". Goodell agreed to meet with Specter, playing down the affair on the eve of the Super Bowl, saying it had not "tainted accomplishments". The pair met in Washington DC in February 2008, with Specter later declaring he "found a lot of questions unanswerable because the tapes and notes had been destroyed".

During the meeting, Goodell alleged that Belichick had told him the Patriots were taping rival coaches' signals since he took on the head coach job in 2000. Goodell continued to defend his actions, insisting that destroying the material was the right course of action and that he had "nothing to hide".

Belichick took responsibility for the incident, declaring, "I misinterpreted the rule … Even though I felt there was a grey area in the rule and I misinterpreted the rule, that was my mistake and we've been penalised for it."

The NFL's Competition Committee backed Goodell's handling of the affair, while Senator Specter told ESPN he felt the league had stonewalled his investigation, alleging his staff had difficulty accessing members of the Patriots and Jets in relation to 'Spygate'. Former Patriots video assistant Matt Walsh provided the NFL with further video from games between 2000 and 2002 in May 2008, but the NFL said no new information came out of those tapes. There were also allegations that the Patriots secretly videoed St Louis Rams' walk-through the day before Super Bowl XXXVI, but these were proved to be unfounded.

The Boston Herald, which initially broke the story of the walkthrough, published an apology to the Patriots and their fans. Specter continued to push for an independent investigation into the entire affair but was shot down by Senator Ted Kennedy, who had the final word on the controversy. "With the war in Iraq raging on, gasoline prices closing in on $4 a gallon, and

Americans losing their homes at record rates to foreclosure, the United States Senate should be focusing on the real problems that Americans are struggling with," Kennedy said … and the affair was consigned to history.

THE ROSIE RUIZ SHORTCUT, 1979

THE BACKGROUND

Rosie Ruiz was born in Cuba in 1953 but moved to the USA with her family when she was just nine years old. In 1973, at age 20, she had a large tumour removed from her head after suffering blackouts. Despite that, she was a promising athlete. She moved to New York to work with a commodities firm and, in 1979, entered the New York Marathon. She finished a respectable 11th in the women's race, with a time just under three hours: 2:56:29. That qualified her to run in the prestigious Boston Marathon and the following April, Ruiz not only won the race, but did so in the remarkable time of 2:31:56. That was the fastest time in the event's long history, and the third best women's marathon time ever recorded.

But something about Ruiz didn't seem quite right. Fellow competitors were covered in sweat and exhausted, while Ruiz was not even panting as she crossed the finish line. Her build was not that of the typical elite marathon runner, with plenty of body fat. And Bill Rodgers, who won the male section of the event, was shocked when he spoke to Ruiz that she knew nothing of the course's interval times and splits, something that was second knowledge to world-class runners. "I asked her about her training and how many intervals she did … she didn't know what intervals were," Rodgers said later. There were also suspicions about Ruiz's remarkable improvement in time from the New York to Boston events – over 25 minutes in less than six months.

THE SCANDAL

Alarm bells began to ring when, after the race, none of the other leading women runners could recall spotting Ruiz on the course. Then two spectators recounted seeing Ruiz charge out of a crowd less than a mile from the finish line, on Commonwealth Avenue. A news photographer, Susan Morrow, then came forward declaring she had met Ruiz during the original New York marathon ... on the subway! Morrow said Ruiz limped across the line in the New York event, claiming to be injured. She was taken for medical attention and marked as having completed the event, thus enabling her to qualify for the Boston marathon. Morrow took no action at the time, but came forward when she watched the finish to the Boston marathon, and saw the same girl who had sat next to her on the subway take first prize.

Officials launched an investigation and after gathering a series of damning testimonies from competitors, spectators and officials, New York officials disqualified Ruiz from the race in 1979, and Boston officials launched their own probe. After some investigating, they stripped Ruiz of the victory, handing first place to Jacqueline Gareau. Three days after the event, the Boston Athletic Association flew Gareau back to Boston, and arranged for a huge crowd to attend as Gareau was photographed crossing the line, now in first place. She was also awarded the winner's medal and answered questions at a press conference. Ranked 22nd before the race, Gareau's 'victory' was the finest moment of her career, but one for which she never received the rightful acclaim – thanks to Rosie Ruiz.

THE AFTERMATH

Shocked and embarrassed by the controversy that made front-page news around the world, officials of both the Boston and New York marathons introduced a host of new, high-tech measures to deter cheating. Video surveillance was brought in, as was transponder timing. Most races now have officials blending in with the crowd, as well as hidden cameras. These have been successfully used to catch cheats in races in several big events since the Ruiz scandal.

Two years after her 2:31:56 minutes of fame, Rosie Ruiz was arrested for allegedly embezzling money from her Manhattan real estate agent employers. A year later, she was again arrested, this time for alleged involvement in a drug deal gone wrong. She was jailed for three weeks and placed on probation. She married in 1984 and divorced in 1986, but still goes by her married name, Rosie Vivas. When questioned, she still insists she ran the Boston Marathon from start to finish in 1980. She never ran competitively again after that day.

More than 30 years later, marathon runner Bill Rodgers can see the humour in the farce. "Rosie Ruiz is the most famous runner of all time," he said. "To the general public and the media, everyone knows about Rosie Ruiz. It's kind of funny."

ASTHMA DRUG CONFUSION DEALS CRUEL BLOW, 1972

THE BACKGROUND

Rick DeMont was born in San Francisco in 1956 and suffered badly with asthma and hayfever as a boy. A doctor told his parents the youngster could improve his health by swimming, so young DeMont took to the pool. He proved himself a more than handy swimmer, too, winning several state titles while still at school. In April of 1972, he stunned officials by coming in third in the US national 1650 metres freestyle event. That performance won DeMont a spot in the US team for the 1972 Olympics when he was just 16 and still at school.

DeMont went to Munich aiming to win gold in the 400 and 1500 metres freestyle events. The International Olympic Committee began its crackdown on drugs in 1972 after several questionable performances at the 1968 Games, and had put out an extensive list of banned substances. DeMont listed his asthma medication, which he had been taking since childhood, on his Olympic paperwork and US medical staff had full knowledge of his condition. But they allegedly failed to clear his prescription with the International Olympic Committee, an oversight that was to have tragic consequences. DeMont won gold in the 400 metres, beating Australia's Brad Cooper by one hundredth of a second, the smallest margin ever in an Olympic event to that time. He was presented with the gold medal and did a routine post-race urine test.

THE SCANDAL

All hell broke loose when DeMont's urine test came back positive for traces of the banned stimulant ephedrine, which was in the asthma medication that he had declared on his medical form. DeMont was stripped of his gold medal, becoming the first American since the legendary

Jim Thorpe in 1913 to suffer such an indignity. He was also barred from the 1500 metres, in which he was the current world champion with a massive chance of another gold medal.

DeMont and many of his team-mates were in tears when the disqualification was made formal. "He has been taking that medication since he was a little boy," DeMont's shattered mother Betty told reporters. The US media called for a review, but the IOC refused to budge. Leading allergy specialist Dr Claude A. Frazier wrote hundreds of letters to officials and the media pointing out that DeMont's asthma medication could in no way have boosted his performance, but they were all ignored. Even US President Richard Nixon took up DeMont's cause. "Your fellow citizens still believe you fairly deserve the gold medal," he wrote in a letter to the swimmer.

DeMont was left bitter and disillusoined. "After Munich I felt like a total loser," he said years later. "I was afraid to face my friends, and all I could think of was, why did this happen to me? I was afraid that every time I got on the starting block people were thinking of me as some kind of speed freak."

THE AFTERMATH

The International Olympic Committee originally decided to leave the gold medal vacant after DeMont was disqualified, but the Australian team protested and Cooper was awarded the gold. As a direct result of the DeMont case, US Olympic officials arranged to have a doctor and a pharmacologist monitor the medications used by their athletes from the 1976 Games.

DeMont made a triumphant return to the pool the following year, at the World Swimming Championships. Under enormous pressure and public scrutiny, he became the first man to swim 400 metres in under four minutes, again beating Cooper in the process. DeMont went on to carve out a fine career as a coach at the University of Arizona, training over 20 US swimming champions. He was inducted into the University's Hall of Fame for his coaching achievements. In 2001, 29 years after his disqualification, the US Olympic Committee cleared Rick DeMont's name. The Committee admitted it did not handle DeMont's medical paperwork properly, leading to his disqualification. The USOC made the apology in the wake of a lawsuit filed by DeMont years earlier. It also amended its official records, which had said DeMont 'did not compete' at the 1972 Olympics.

"I think he's very pleased," DeMont's attorney, David Ulich, said of the news. "He's anxious to have his name cleared and to be putting this behind him so he can move on with his life." Despite several appeals to the IOC, DeMont has never got his gold medal back, but lives in hope that one day, he will see it returned to its rightful owner.

AGASSI COMES CLEAN, 2009

THE BACKGROUND

Andre Agassi was among the most popular and charismatic players in tennis history. A brilliant ground-stroker, he enjoyed a lengthy career through the 1980s, 1990s and 2000s. He was seen as a leading light in the sport's resurgence in the 1990s after several years in the doldrums, with young fans flocking to watch him around the world. Adding to his star power was his marriage to actress Brooke Shield from 1997 to 1999.

A graduate of the Nick Bolletieri Tennis Academy in Florida, Agassi turned pro in 1986 at just 16 and won an instant following with his mullet hairstyle and colourful clothing. He refused to play at Wimbledon early in his career because of the event's conservative culture and white dress code. Agassi finally made his Wimbledon debut in 1991 and the following year, won the title to claim his first grand slam. He went on to play 15 grand slam finals, winning eight, and won a gold medal at the 1996 Atlanta Olympics. He is one of only seven players to win all four grand slam majors.

Injuries and lack of form saw his world ranking plummet to number 147 in 1997, with critics claiming he was a spent force. But Agassi won a spot in tennis folklore by regaining his world number one ranking just two years later before finally retiring due to a series of nagging back injuries in 2006.

THE SCANDAL

In 2009, Agassi released a tell-all autobiography, entitled *Open*. In it, he made the startling confession that he used the recreational drug methamphetamine (crystal meth) in 1997. In a worrying revelation, Agassi also declared that he confessed the drug use to tennis authorities after failing a drug test, lied about the circumstances, and escaped any punishment. Agassi claimed he was introduced to the drug by an assistant, "Slim", whom he later fired.

Agassi spoke of his sadness and regret at dabbling into the world of drugs. Recalling how it all began, he said, "Slim dumps a small pile of powder on the coffee table. He cuts it, snorts it. He cuts it again. I snort some. Then comes a tidal wave of euphoria that sweeps away every negative thought in my head. I've never felt so alive, so hopeful – and I've never felt such energy."

Agassi was in the midst of his worst season at the time, and saw the drug as an escape. Soon afterwards, a tennis official told Agassi he had failed a drug test. "My name, my career, everything is now on the line," he recalled. "Whatever I've achieved, whatever I've worked for, might soon mean nothing. Days later I sit in a hard-backed chair, a legal pad in my lap, and write a letter to the ATP. It's filled with lies interwoven with bits of truth. I say Slim, whom I've since fired, is a known drug user, and that he often spikes his sodas with meth, which is true. Then I come to the central lie of the letter. I say that recently I drank accidentally from one of Slim's spiked sodas, unwittingly ingesting his drugs. I ask for understanding and leniency and hastily sign it: Sincerely. I feel ashamed, of course. I promise myself that this lie is the end of it."

THE AFTERMATH

The ATP chose to believe Agassi's excuse after reviewing his case. While the minimum ban for recreational drug use is three months, Agassi was let off and charges were withdrawn.

The International Tennis Federation declared it was "surprised and disappointed" by Agassi's revelation in his book. It also led to questions about how many other players had been caught failing drug tests, only for the results to be swept under the carpet. "I think it will have underlying implications for the sport in terms of the suspicion about some of the athletes and whether or not they are on drugs," BBC correspondent Jonathan Overend commented. "The fact that Agassi lied and the authorities believed him has enormous repercussions. How many other cases may there have been like this?"

The scandal when the book came out was brief, and did not affect Agassi's popularity. The star is married to fellow tennis great Steffi Graf and the pair are regarded as tennis royalty. Agassi's legacy, the Andre Agassi Charitable Foundation, has raised over $60 million for at-risk children.

The drug use wasn't the only major revelation in the book. Agassi also revealed that his trademark mullet, which won him thousands of teenybopper fans, was a wig.

AUSTRALIAN FOOTBALL STAR POISONED, 1953

THE BACKGROUND

A speedy winger, Bobby Lulham was a star in Australian Rugby League in the 1940s and early 1950s. Born in Newcastle in 1926, he joined the Balmain club in Sydney as a professional in 1947 and set a record for most tries by a rookie, with 28 in his first year. He helped Balmain win the grand final that season, and within 12 months had won a spot in the New South Wales state and Australian teams.

Lulham had the football world at his feet but midway through the 1953 season, he complained of pains in his feet and numbness in his legs. He turned out for the Tigers against Canterbury at Leichhardt Oval one Sunday afternoon, but played poorly and looked sluggish. The next day, he reported for work as a boilermaker before returning home, feeling sick. To make matters worse, his hair began falling out.

Lulham was admitted to Royal Prince Alfred Hospital in Sydney, after complaining of feeling ill for more than a week, and doctors began tests. His wife was too distressed to speak to the media, but his mother-in-law, Veronica Monty, told the local newspaper: "I'm sure no one has anything against him. He is very popular with everyone."

THE SCANDAL

Doctors made a startling discovery after performing tests – Lulham had doses of rat poison in his system. A woman phoned the doctor treating Lulham, as well as Detective Sergeant George Davis, claiming she knew who poisoned the star, before hanging up. Within weeks, police charged Veronica Monty with attempting to kill Lulham by lacing a cup of Milo (hot chocolate) with rat poison. They also believed it was Monty who had made the anonymous phone calls.

In a court case that rocked the conservative Sydney scene in the 1950s, they established that Monty had engaged in a sexual relationship with her son-in-law while her daughter was at church on Sundays. Monty then attempted to murder Lulham so her daughter would not find out about the affair. Huge crowds attended court each day to hear lurid details of the affair, mainly consisting of women, who brought their own cut lunches for a day's entertainment. They heard that Monty had separated from her husband recently, moving in with Bob and Judith Lulham. Monty confessed to poisoning Lulham, but said she was depressed at the time and attempted to take her own life before giving Lulham the poisoned cup by mistake. "I must have picked up the wrong cup," she said. "I really thought I was going to get the poison."

The crown prosecutor, Mr Charles Rooney, launched a fierce attack on Monty and Lulham, declaring the case "demonstrated beyond all doubt that a most infamous and unnatural relationship of sexual nature existed between the pair". He called the affair a "disgraceful episode" and one in which "the guilty pair polluted the marital bed". Despite all this, Monty was found not guilty by a jury and was released.

THE AFTERMATH

In 1954, 10 months after the court case, Judith Lulham filed for divorce from her husband Bobby, naming her mother as the co-respondent. At nearly the same time, Alfred Monty filed for divorce from wife Veronica, naming her son-in-law, Bobby Lulham, as the co-respondent in his suit.

Veronica Monty took on an assumed name and worked as a maid in a Sydney motel after the case. In 1955, she took a pistol belonging to the motel's owner and shot herself dead. Lulham never played football again due to the effects of the rat poison on his body. He died in 1986, aged 60.

The case was one of nearly a dozen in Australia in the early 1950s in which women were charged with poisoning family members with Thall-rat, a rodent killer freely available at department stores and found in thousands of homes around the country. Because it was tasteless and odourless, it was an effective way for women to free themselves of unwanted husbands or family members. In one famous case around the same time, a Sydney grandmother murdered four members of her family with baked treats laced with thallium and attempted to murder another three. She was sentenced to life in prison.

As a result of the poisoning spree, the Australian government banned the unrestricted sale of thallium in 1952. An Australian documentary film on the killings, *Recipe for Murder*, was released in 2001.

LITTLE LEAGUE OVER-AGE SCANDAL, 2001

THE BACKGROUND

Danny Almonte was born in Moca, in the Dominican Republic, in 1987. Before his 14th birthday, he would become the most famous (or, many would argue, infamous) teenager in the United States. Danny's parents, Felipe and Sonia, were great lovers of baseball, a major sport in the Dominican Republic. Felipe founded a youth league in their hometown, but in 1994, the family moved to America. They eventually settled in the Bronx, where Danny began a promising baseball career. Taller and stronger than many of his team-mates, Danny proved a formidable pitcher. He had a high leg lift and his fastball had been clocked at up to 75 miles per hour – far too hot for most 12-year-olds to handle. At five foot eight inches tall, he was compared to the great Randy Johnson. Pressmen who had dubbed Johnson 'The Big Unit' soon referred to Danny as 'The Little Unit'.

There were suspicions Danny was older than his team-mates in the Roland Paulino All Stars, but this was not uncommon in Little League. In the mid-Atlantic regional finals in 2001, Danny threw a no-hitter against the Pennsylvania State College team. That win earned the boys from the Bronx a spot in the Little League World Series, and they became the darlings of New York.

THE SCANDAL

Four days later, Danny threw the first perfect game the Little League World Series had seen in over 30 years, as the Bronx Baby Boomers, as they became known, romped to an easy win against a team from Apopka, Florida. In the return game, Danny was ineligible to pitch, having thrown the entire game the day before, and the Baby Boomers were defeated. But Danny finished the tournament with 62 strikeouts of the 72 batters he faced, and the team was honoured for its third-place finish by being presented to the crowd at a Yankees game. Mayor Rudi Giuliani even gave them with a key to the city.

Behind the scenes, rival teams were certain Danny was more than 12 years old. A couple went as far as hiring private investigators to look into the matter, but were unable to turn up any hard evidence. *Sports Illustrated* magazine then sent a reporter to Danny's hometown of Moca soon after the World Series. He found civil records that proved that Danny was in fact born in 1987, not 1989 as his parents had claimed. The magazine published its findings, prompting a massive inquiry by the Little League. Danny's parents denied the claims, declaring they had a handwritten birth certificate to show he really was born in 1989. The document proved to be a forgery, with the head of the Dominican public records office holding his own inquiry before declaring Danny's real birthdate was in 1987.

THE AFTERMATH

As soon as Danny's real age was confirmed, officials acted swiftly. They retroactively disqualified him from the tournament and stripped his team of all their wins. Their records were removed from official tournament records and they were forced to demonstrate full compliance with Little League rules and show all players' birth certificates before being allowed to compete the following year. Danny's father Felipe Almonte was banned from any association with Little League baseball for life. League president Rolando Paulino was also suspended as, under Little League rules, he was the man responsible for player eligibility. In the Dominican Republic, Felipe Almonte was charged with falsifying a birth certificate.

Danny Almonte was absolved of any wrongdoing, with officials declaring he knew nothing of the ruse and believed he really was born in 1989. Back in New York, welfare officials found that Danny had not attended school in 2000–01, a violation of state law that could result in him being placed in foster care.

Danny moved to Florida for a while and continued to play junior baseball. In 2005, aged 18, he married a 30-year-old woman. He tried out for the Major League in 2006 but missed out. The following year he played in the Illinois Frontier League with little success. He gave up pitching when arm soreness became chronic, and played for some time as an outfielder. He eventually returned to New York, volunteering as an assistant coach at his former school, James Monroe High, working on an unpaid basis. "He's giving back to the team, to the community," school coach Mike Turo said. "He doesn't want a dime. He wants to help these kids. That's what he wants to be known for – not the stuff in the past."

PIQUET'S ALLEGED CRASH ORDERS, 2008

THE BACKGROUND

Nelson Piquet Jr was born into car racing royalty. His father, Nelson Piquet, was one of Brazil's greatest ever drivers and a three-time winner of the Formula One world championship. After winning the GP2 series in 2005 in Belgium and finishing in second place in the GP2 series in 2006, he signed with the Renault team as a test driver in Formula One in 2007. By 2008, Renault promoted the impressive Piquet Jr, then aged 23, to its race team, alongside Spaniard Fernando Alonso.

Piquet's vehicle being removed from the track.

The stable's shining star was Alonso, who won world championships in 2005 and 2006. Renault had only re-entered Formula One in 2000, when it bought the Benetton Formula One team. In 2008, Renault had not won a race in over two years and was rumoured to be considered pulling out of the sport.

The 2008 Singapore Grand Prix was the sport's first night race, and Renault struggled in qualifying, with Alonso starting 15th and Piquet Jr 16th.

THE SCANDAL

Midway through the race, Piquet Jr hit the wall at turn 17, a spot where there was no nearby crane, forcing a safety car to be deployed. Brazil's Felipe Massa was leading at the time, but under new rules, the pit lane was closed until all vehicles had been picked up by the safety car, resulting in Massa and the other lead drivers losing their advantage. They rejoined the race at the end of the queue. Some drivers also had to stop while the pits were closed so as not to run out of fuel, and were penalised as a result. So many of the leaders found themselves suddenly behind Alonso, who had already pitted early in the race, with slower drivers making it difficult to pass them on the narrow track. Alonso took the lead in the final stages of the race and held on to win. Some cynics questioned Renault's good fortune, but with no hard evidence, no action was taken.

In August 2009, Renault dropped Piquet Jr from their team and soon afterwards reports emerged that Piquet Jr had been ordered to crash in Singapore. The Federation Internationale de l'Automobile ordered an inquiry and accused Renault of interfering with the race outcome by causing a deliberate crash. Piquet Jr told FIA that Renault Managing Director Flavio Briatore and Executive Director of Engineering Pat Symonds ordered him to crash at a specified corner.

Renault F1 declared it intended to take legal action against Piquet Jr for false allegations and blackmail. Piquet won a libel case against Renault in 2010, receiving a full apology.

THE AFTERMATH

Days after the initial charges, Renault FI announced both Briatore and Symonds were no longer part of their team and the charges would not be contested. The World Motorsports Council disqualified Renault F1, but suspended the sentence for two years. Briatore was banned indefinitely and Symonds ousted for five years.

The scandal deeply damaged the sport's image. Racing legend Sir Jackie Charlton declared: "There is something fundamentally rotten and wrong at the heart of Formula One. Never in my experience has Formula One been in such a mood of self-destruction." Another great, Nikki Lauda, called it "the biggest damage (to Formula One) ever." The respected British newspaper *The Times* labelled the incident "the worst single piece of cheating in the history of sport" because of the potentially lethal consequences involved.

Renault's main sponsors, ING and Mutua Madrilena, both ended their deals days after the findings, ordering their logos to be stripped from the team's cars. Briatore announced his plan to sue FIA and early in 2010, France's Tribunal de Grande Instance overturned his ban. Symonds' suspension was also ended. The FIA declared it would appeal the decision and months later announced it had reached a settlement with the pair, with Briatore and Symonds both agreeing not to work in Formula One until 2013.

Piquet Jr also questioned whether Alonso knew of the plan, in the light of his unusual race plan of starting with a low fuel level before an early pit stop. But Alonso denied any knowledge of the conspiracy and was cleared by FIA.

TENNIS TANKING FEARS, 2007

THE BACKGROUND

Russian Nikolay Davydenko has been one of world tennis' best-known and most consistent players since the year 2000. Born in the Ukraine in 1981, he moved to Russia when just 11 years old, where he lived with elder brother Eduard, a tennis coach. He turned professional in 1999, aged just 18, and has reached the semi-finals of four grand slam events. He has won three ATP Masters series and by 2006 was ranked the third-best player in the world.

The following year, in the 2007 Polish Open in Sopot, Davydenko was playing a second-round match against Argentina's little-known Martin Vassallo Arguello and won the first set easily, as expected, 6-2. But Davydenko was complaining about a foot injury he'd suffered in the first round and lost the second set 6-3. He was trailing 2-1 in the third when he retired hurt, handing Arguello a spot in the quarter-finals. It was Davydenko's third loss in the first round since having made the fourth round at Wimbledon a month earlier.

Nikolay Davydenko on the tennis court in 2007.

"I had problems with my foot in the first round," he said. "I must think about other important tournaments. I don't want to aggravate the injury. Normally I try to fight to the end but it was very painful and I may have done even more damage by trying to finish the match. Since the beginning of Monday I've had a problem with my left toes. Today that became a problem with my foot. In the second set it was very painful and I couldn't run the way I normally do."

THE SCANDAL

Soon afterwards, tennis officials announced they were investigating what they termed "suspicious betting patterns" on the match. In an unprecedented move, English gambling company Betfair declared all bets on the Davydenko-Arguello game to be void. The company received over $7 million in bets on the match –10 times the usual amount, including several huge wagers from Russia – with almost all of it on Arguello to win, even after Davydenko won the first set.

Players and officials were stunned by the implications. "You try to leave it to the players to play the game the right way," said US superstar Andy Roddick. "I think we expect that of them. If something's found that's shady, I, for one, will be extremely [ticked] off. Obviously you want to wait and see it play out, but it's too bad that it only takes one idiot to ruin things and create a bad story." But Arguello defended Davydenko: "I don't think that [Davydenko] has something to do with this," Arguello said Friday. "I was playing against him, but he was playing also with an injury, and that's all that I know about the match, and that's also what I felt in the match. I felt nothing else."

Betfair, who had made a deal with the ATP four years earlier to share information on any irregular betting activity, said it was worried by the volume of wagers on Arguello from the start. "We think the market quite clearly wasn't fair," Betfair managing director Mark Davies said. "The prices seemed very odd. As a result, in the interest of fairness and integrity and in consultation with the ATP, we have decided to void the market and return all stakes to [bettors]." It was the first time Betfair took such action in any sport. "The ATP takes issues surrounding gambling extremely seriously," the men's tour said in a statement. "We are committed to ensuring our sport remains corruption free."

THE AFTERMATH

The incident quickly made Davydenko's life hell, even as he protested his innocence. "I've never gambled in my life and I don't know any guys who do," he said. "It's difficult – it's like mentally you are tired, not physically. It would be good for me to take a rest and nobody hear nothing about me. It's pretty tough for me in this position now. Everybody sees I am like bad guy who is gambling. I've never done anything in my life like this. I try to say every week I don't do anything like this. I never did. How many weeks will I have to answer questions? How many months?"

British star Andy Murray weighed into the debate, saying that although it was difficult to prove players guilty of "tanking" in matches, "everyone knows it goes on".

Nearly a year later, in September 2008, the ATP cleared Davydenko and Arguello of match-fixing. In the meantime, Davydenko found himself embroiled in a new controversy, and was was fined $2,000 by the ATP for "not trying hard enough" in the 2007 St Petersburg Open. But Davydenko appealed against the fine and was successful in having it overturned. Despite the controversies, he remains one of the leading players on the world scene.

BASEBALL'S DIRTY SECRET EXPOSED, 2005

THE BACKGROUND

The use of chemicals in baseball didn't start in the 1990s; way back in the 1880s, pitcher Pud Galvin was said to have been a regular user of an elixir composed of the testicles of domestic animals, which supposedly gave him extra energy, and there were rumours the legendary Babe Ruth was injected with an extract derived from sheep testicles. Many players who served in World War II, where they were given amphetamines, continued to use them when they returned home, in the major leagues. Tom House, a pitcher for Atlanta, Boston Red Sox and Seattle in the 1970s, later admitted to using steroids "they wouldn't give to horses". And he insisted plenty of his team-mates and opponents were also "juiced up". At a series of drug trials in Pittsburgh in the 1980s, several players admitted to the use of amphetamines in

Alex Rodriguez, in the field for the New York Yankees in 2008.

the game. Some players just experimented with drugs to see if it would give them a much-needed edge; others were regular users. It was a dark secret in the game, which those involved spoke little about. But the murmurs and whispers became a storm that hit the game, when a series of damning revelations came to light in the 2000s.

THE SCANDAL

Former star slugger Jose Canseco got the ball rolling in 2005, writing a book, *Juiced*, which rocked baseball to its foundations. Home run totals had begun to soar in the mid-1990s, raising suspicion about steroids. Canseco declared that many of MLB's biggest names were regular steroid users, claims that were quickly denied by those involved. Three years later, Canseco wrote a second book, *Vindicated*, outlining his frustrations over the furore caused by his original claims. He further named Alex Rodriguez as a steroid user.

MLB was forced to investigate and a stunned public was told that over 100 of the game's biggest players had tested positive for banned substances. The game received a further body-blow early in 2010, when record-breaking slugger Mark McGwire admitted to steroid use. This ignited a furious debate in the game: should McGwire's historic feat in 1998, when he broke Roger Maris' record for most home runs in a season, be thrown out of the record books? Several players were found to be using androstenedione, a substance banned by the International Olympic Committee.

Leading players found themselves under massive scrutiny. Another record-breaker, Barry Bonds, was linked to the scandal. In 2005, US Congress called in a host of big-name players, including Bonds, Canseco, Rodriguez, McGwire and Sammy Sosa. The hearings painted a picture of regular use of steroids by many stars. Baseball commissioner Bud Selig ordered an investigation into the scandal in 2006. The Bay Area Laboratory Co-Operative (BALCO) was revealed to have supplied drugs to a number of players.

Bonds admitted to taking steroids, but claimed they were given to him by his personal trainer, who had told him the drugs were flaxseed oil and arthritis cream. In 2011, Bonds was sentenced to 30 days house arrest on one count of obstruction of justice.

THE AFTERMATH

The Mitchell Report, a 409-page document, was released in December 2007 as a result of Selig's investigation, naming 89 MLB stars who used steroids and other performance-enhancing drugs. The author, Democrat Senator George J. Mitchell, slammed the MLB Players Association for being "largely un-cooperative". Mitchell alleged that at least one player from each of the 30 MLB teams took performance-enhancing drugs. He recommended that MLB should employ an independent testing firm to improve their testing program. He also advocated greater education of players about health concerns related to drugs and their side effects. He found that MLB's 2002 crackdown on drugs resulted in many players switching to undetectable human growth hormones. He blamed not only the players, but the entire baseball community for the epidemic, with many within the game turning a blind eye to the problem. Selig labelled the report a "call to action" and declared, "I will act."

Drug testing radically changed after the report, with MLB becoming far stricter. Random testing became much more common and the range of drugs tested for was greatly increased. In 2009, Yankees great Alex Rodriguez admitted he took drugs between 2001 and 2003 when he played for the Texas Rangers, claiming he was "naive" and "stupid" and that baseball had a "different culture" then.

Many of baseball's biggest players of the era continue to insist they never took performance-enhancing drugs.

SAILOR'S TRAGIC HOAX, 1968

THE BACKGROUND

Born in India in 1932, Donald Crowhurst moved to England in his childhood and was forced to leave school early following the death of his father. He began a cadetship with the air force and became a pilot, but quit the RAF after allegedly being caught in an embarrassing position with an officer's daughter. He then joined the army, but also left after finding it was not to his liking.

Crowhurst began his own business, inventing a radio direction finder for boats and naming it the Navicator. The revolutionary device allowed users to get their bearings on marine and radio beacons with a handheld device. But Crowhurst experienced financial problems, and it was then that he developed a daring scheme to get rich. Crowhurst decided to enter the Golden Globe Race, an around-the-world solo sailing challenge covering a gruelling 27,000 miles. He believed that winning the race would provide him with much-needed cash in the form of prize money and sponsorship, and also gain publicity for the Navicator. Crowhurst opted to attempt the challenge in a trimaran, a fast boat, but one that experts believed was unsuitable in the dangerous waters of the Atlantic Ocean. He mortgaged his house to pay for the boat to be built, and eventually set sail on 31 October 1968.

THE SCANDAL

Crowhurst immediately encountered problems, his boat being ill-prepared and his own sailing skills limited. The danger signs were there for all to see; his boat, *Teignmouth Electron*, encountered teething troubles, and Crowhurst suffered a bad case of sea-sickness just sailing through calm waters to the starting line. But he pressed on, determined to make a name for himself despite the clear danger signals.

After just a few weeks, he faced a gut-wrenching choice, either to turn home and face embarrassment and financial ruin, or to plough on and risk losing the boat (and his life). But late in November, he decided on an alternative – to linger in the south Atlantic for months, undetected, while the other boats continued on their way, falsify his logs and then rejoin the race on the home leg.

He cut back his radio reports, at times going weeks without giving his position, and was often vague when he came on air. For weeks his own wife did not know if he was dead or alive. His plan was to finish the race behind the leaders, thus avoiding close scrutiny of his logbooks, which would reveal him to be a brazen fraud. At one stage, he even made a stop on dry land in South America to make running repairs on his boat, a blatant breach of race rules. But because he was supposed to be thousands of miles away, he was never detected. He told puzzled local Argentinian officials that he was taking part in a regatta.

By early December, when he resumed radio contact, he found himself the new race favourite because of his position, being cheered on by millions of fans. His log books later showed his state of mind to be erratic. When his wife sent him a telegram that he looked set to win the race, he appeared to lose what was left of his sanity.

THE AFTERMATH

Crowhurst was never seen or heard of again after a radio transmission in late June. His last log entry on 1 July 1969 showed his distress. "It is finished, it is finished," he wrote. "It is the mercy, it is the end of my game. The truth has been revealed."

Some 10 days later, his boat was found by a British Royal Mail ship, abandoned near the Azores Islands. For years afterwards, there were alleged sightings of Crowhurst, with his family clinging to hope he was still alive. One man claimed to have seen him in Scotland, while someone forged a message that Crowhurst was supposed to have sent in a bottle. An inquest into his disappearance, after his log books and papers were read, came to the conclusion that he had a mental breakdown and probably threw himself overboard and drowned.

His deception has become the stuff of legend, dramatised in several movies and plays and also the subject of a book. The eventual winner of the race, Robin Knox-Johnston, donated his £5,000 pound prize money to Crowhurst's widow and children, enabling them to keep the family home he had worked so hard to save.

Clare Crowhurst revealed years later that the night before setting sail, her late husband broke down in tears, realising the dangers ahead. But she has continued to defend the disgraced sailor's reputation. "The man who went to sea would have never thought of cheating," she said. "But who knows what somebody goes through when they can't reach out and touch someone and receive human warmth."

ASSAULT IN THE RING, 1983

THE BACKGROUND

Born in Puerto Rico in 1955, Luis Resto had a troubled childhood. After moving to New York at the age of nine, he allegedly assaulted his math teacher at school, spending six months in a facility for the mentally disturbed as a result. Like many 'lost' youngsters, he took to boxing as a way to handle his aggressive tendencies. Resto, although he was a light puncher, was quick on his feet and found early success. He won two New York Golden Gloves titles as a welterweight and came close to winning Olympic selection for the USA in 1976. He turned professional the following year, scoring a first-up points defeat of Julio Chevalier. He won his first seven bouts and quickly climbed to 10th in the world rankings, earning a fight against undefeated Billy Collins Jnr in 1983 at Madison Square Garden, on the undercard to a Roberto Duran match. Resto gave Collins a dreadful pounding, winning a unanimous point decision in a major upset. Collins finished in terrible shape, with both eyes swollen shut and his face distorted and bloodied.

THE SCANDAL

Seconds after the verdict, Collins' trainer, his father Billy Sr, went to shake Resto's hand and immediately realised there was something very wrong. Resto's gloves felt thin, and Collins Sr screamed to officials that some of the padding had been removed. The gloves were seized and the New York Boxing Commission ordered an investigation. After a month of interviews and inquiries, the NYBC declared that Resto's trainer, Panama Lewis, had taken the padding out of Resto's gloves. Slits were found at the bottom of each glove, through which the padding had been removed. The inquiry also blamed Resto, alleging he should have known the gloves had been tampered with.

Resto's boxing licence was suspended for at least a year. Three years later, in 1986, both Resto and Lewis were put on trial for the incident, charged with assault, criminal possession of a weapon – Resto's hands – as well as conspiracy. Prosecutors found there was a massive plunge in betting on Resto shortly before the fight and speculated that it played a role in the pair's actions. Resto was found guilty and served two and a half years in jail. Lewis was sentenced to six years, serving more than three. Both were banned from boxing for life.

THE AFTERMATH

Collins never fought again, suffering permanently blurred vision from the incident. Months after the fight, he suffered a car crash while intoxicated in his home state of Tennessee. Collins died upon impact when his car smashed into a creek. Touted as a future world champion before the fateful bout with Resto, he was just 22 years of age. Family members believe that Collins, distraught at his boxing career ending and the extent of his injuries, may have taken his own life.

Collins Sr was adamant Resto knew of the deceit. "You don't think Resto knew he didn't have padding in the gloves?" he told *Sports Illustrated* in 1998. "You don't think Panama Lewis took it out? I've had 15 years to think about it and I know – I know – they did it." Resto tried to regain his license for nearly 20 years and was eventually allowed to work as a cornerman. He worked in a variety of odd jobs and lived for years in a basement apartment gym where he used to train in his youth. After years of denials, Resto finally admitted he knew Lewis had taken the padding out of his gloves. In 2007, he publicly apologised to Collins' widow, Andrea Collins-Nile, who was suing the state of New York for failing to protect her late husband. Resto also made the shock revelation that Lewis soaked his hands in plaster of Paris before the fight to make his fists even harder. Resto admitted going along with the plan. "I said 'Let's go ahead and do it.' At the time I was young . . . I went along," Resto confessed.

He also admitted that Lewis mixed asthma medicine with his water to give his lungs greater power in fights. Mrs Collins-Nile, when told of the confession, commented, "Ultimately I'm not Luis Resto's judge." Lewis has never admitted any guilt, insisting the fight was clean and claiming that a mystery man removed the padding from Resto's gloves after the fight. He insisted it was his cornerman, Artie Curley, who wrapped Resto's hands before the fight. While Resto went on to work odd jobs, Lewis recovered from the scandal to own several houses. "Panama, he can go to hell . . . f**ck Panama," a bitter Resto said, years later.

WAR ON THE PITCH, 1969

THE BACKGROUND

Honduras and El Salvador were troubled neighbours in Central America back in the 1960s. There was simmering tension between the two countries over land reform and immigration that saw bickering between rival politicians and even some minor border skirmishes. Honduras was five times larger than El Salvador, but at the time, El Salvador's population was more than double that of its neighbour. In fact, with 400 people per square mile, El Salvador was one of the most densely populated countries in its hemisphere. For much of the 20th century, large groups of Salvadorans had migrated across the border, their number estimated to be around 300,000 by the 1960s. Many were peasants, and their dreams of owning land were made harder by political pressure from the rich to keep Honduran property in the hands of Hondurans.

The Hondurans reclaimed land that had been illegally occupied by Salvadorian immigrants under new land reforms in the mid-1960s, increasing tension between the two groups. Honduras resented the newcomers and expelled many Salvadorans, both those who had come looking for work and those who had been long-term residents. Many Salvadorans married Hondurans and those couples came under particular pressure. The two countries argued over immigration throughout the period and a two-year accord, struck in 1967, was not renewed when it expired early in 1969, adding tension to the region.

THE SCANDAL

With these political issues creating a dramatic backdrop, the two countries played a FIFA World Cup soccer qualifying game in the Honduran capital Tegucigalpa in June 1969. With fans fighting on the streets and in the grandstands, the scores were locked at nil-all, before Honduras scored a late winner. The goal came in time added on for injuries, and the Salvadorans felt they had been cheated. Tensions were running so high leading into the return match in El Salvador a week later that the Salvadoran team was hidden by police security before the game. The Honduran flag and anthem were booed, there was rioting in the streets and three spectators were killed.

El Salvador turned the tables on home soil, winning 3-0. The Honduran fans who had travelled to the game had a traumatic trip home, with locals pelting their cars with rocks, smashing windscreens and causing some injuries. There were also unconfirmed reports that several Hondurans were being held as prisoners after fighting between rival fans. Honduran refugees poured over the Salvadoran border, telling tales of atrocities. Salvadoran shops in Tegucigalpa were attacked. Meanwhile, the teams played a third game, on neutral ground in Mexico City, with El Salvador winning 3-2. The game was again fiery and on the same day the two countries moved a step closer to war, breaking off diplomatic relations with one another.

THE AFTERMATH

On 14 July, a few weeks after the final game, Honduran planes bombed and strafed Salvadoran targets. El Salvador quickly replied, bombing Tegucigalpa's airport and other military outposts. The next day, the Honduran air force, stronger than that of its neighbour, retaliated with a strike on the San Salvador airport, as well as the port town of Acajutla. Planes also engaged in dogfights. Salvadoran ground troops crossed the border as the fighting escalated, capturing a series of towns. It was a delicate balance, with the Hondurans controlling the air and the Salvadorans superior on the ground, and both sides fast running out of bullets.

Both countries asked the United States for arms and aid and were refused flat. What the US did do, through the Organisation of American States, was exert pressure on both sides to end the fighting. A cease-fire was agreed for 10pm on 18 July, four days and five hours after the conflict began. But in that short time, over 3,000 people were killed on both sides, soldiers and civilians. It was 11 years before the two nations signed a peace treaty in 1980, which in effect ensured that all future battles between the unfriendly neighbours would remain on the football field.

WOMEN 'INVADE' LORD'S, 1998

THE BACKGROUND

The spiritual home of cricket for over 200 years, the Marylebone Cricket Club at Lord's found itself under siege in 1999. The club, located in London, is regarded as the biggest brand in world cricket and for many years the club was actually the game's governing body. The MCC remains the copyright holder of the Laws of Cricket and reissues them when it feels the need arises. It schedules regular fixtures and has over 20,000 members, many of whom are among the most influential people in England.

But in 1999, the MCC found itself under fire, because it emerged that of these 20,000-plus members, not one was female. The club remained one of the last bastions of male chauvinism, continually refusing to allow women to become members. In two centuries, just one woman (other than staff members) had ever entered the Lord's Pavilion during games – Queen Elizabeth II. Ironically, the Queen is the club's patron.

In February 1998, some 56 percent of members voted to allow women to be accepted into the cub. But, under the Lord's constitution, a two-thirds majority is required to make changes to the bylaws, and the move was defeated. This only added to the pressure on the club, with British Prime Minister Tony Blair slamming Lord's as being "out of touch". The club responded by commissioning a poll of members and enlisting influential figures, including former England captain David Gower and Sir Paul Getty, to push the case for women.

THE SCANDAL

Desperate to project a more modern-day image in the lead-up to the 1999 World Cup, the club held a second vote only months later in 1998. The club's push also had a commercial motive – sponsors were shunning the club because of its sexist policy and the publicity it was attracting. It is estimated the second vote cost the club over £75,000, and the mere fact that the vote was taken so soon after being defeated infuriated many members. "I think the new vote is appalling," one member complained. "It's like the government losing a general election and losing because of their policies and then saying they would like another vote because they didn't explain them properly."

Despite the objections, a second vote was taken in September 1998 and this time, nearly 70 percent of the 13,500 members who voted were in favour of ending the ban on women. "It is without doubt an historic moment," MCC president Tony Lewis said. Five women were invited to join as a consequence, the first being Lucy Mullens, a 24-year-old physical education teacher who had been playing cricket for the past seven years. Because of its new 'open' policy, the Marylebone Cricket Club was now eligible to receive funding grants from the National Lottery, a privilege it was previously denied because of its policy of segregation. The club pledged to induct 10 honorary members within the year, who would not have to go on the waiting list, which could take up to 20 years. The club also spoke of a plan to create an all-women's MCC team. Then England captain Rachael Heyhoe Flint described it as "a wonderful day for women".

THE AFTERMATH

The 3,600 women, 374,000 primary schoolgirls and 83,000 secondary schoolgirls who play cricket in Britain saw the verdict as a major victory, along with feminists throughout the world. While the ruling was seen as popular in the general public, it was condemned by many of the 'old guard' within Lord's. Members voiced their disapproval at a special general meeting held shortly after the results of the vote were announced. They insisted that one bar in the Lord's pavilion remain for men only, "on an experimental basis".

Lewis fired back at the critics, denying Lord's had become a victim of political correctness. "The thinking of the committee was simple – we could not claim to be a great cricket club unless we had a women's team and women members," he said. A decade after the historic vote, however, women were still very much in the minority at Lord's. The club had 62 female members in 2008, roughly 0.3 percent of the overall membership of over 18,000. That minute number drew an angry rebuke from Dr Katherine Rake, director of the Fawcett Society, a group that campaigns for equality. "Paying lip service to equality is not enough," she said. "Funders and sponsors should be looking at how they're delivering equality as well." Chief Executive of England's Women's Sport and Fitness Foundation, Sue Tibballs, added, "The case of the MCC shows that it isn't enough to just open the door; more needs to be done to remove the hurdles and invite women to walk through it."

ROY JONES JR ROBBED, 1988

THE BACKGROUND

Roy Jones Jr was born in Pensacola, Florida, in 1969 and had a tough upbringing. His father, Roy Sr, was a ruthless taskmaster and punished his son for the smallest infractions of his strict rules. "I was in pain all day, every day," Jones recalled years later. "I was so scared of my father."

But Roy Sr also gave the youngster a valuable lesson in life – he taught him how to fight. He ran his own gym, training young fighters and pushing his son to the limit. At 15, Roy Jr won the US National Junior title (54kg division) and three years later, he took out the National Golden Gloves (71kg division). That earned him a spot on the US team for the 1988 Seoul Olympics, and he breezed through his opening rounds. Blessed with fast feet and a lethal left hook, he won his four bouts in clinical fashion to progress to the gold medal match against local hopeful Park Si-Hun. Park was a capable fighter, but in contrast to Jones, had to fight hard to reach the final. There were claims along the way that only favourable treatment from the judges in at least two of his bouts had enabled Park to get that far, and with that in mind, the American went into the final as firm favourite.

THE SCANDAL

The final itself went pretty much to script. Jones was too strong and fast for the local fighter, winning the bout by a commanding score of 86 to 32. Jones rarely raised a sweat and did enough to convince everyone in the arena that the gold medal was his. But remarkably, as the fighters went to centre ring for the decision, it emerged that the five judges were handing the bout – and the gold medal – to Park, by 3-2.

The referee, Aldo Leoni was stunned. As he raised a sheepish Park's hand, he whispered to Jones, "I can't believe they are doing this to you." Park himself allegedly apologised. Jones was stunned, unable to comprehend what had just happened.

One judge, Hiouad Larbi of Morocco, later admitted he voted for Park because he felt so sorry for the South Korean being humiliated in front of his home crowd. "It was a terrible thing," he said. "The American won easily. So easily I was positive my four fellow judges would score the fight for him by a wide margin. So I voted for the Korean to make the score only 4-1 and not embarrass the home country."

At the award ceremony, an embarrassed Park, standing in the gold medal spot on the podium, held Jones' fist aloft. Jones accepted his silver medal with dignity, despite calls that he should boycott the ceremony in protest. Jones grabbed an interpreter, fronted Park, and asked him if he had in fact won the fight. Park replied, "No." Jones held no grudge against Park. "I don't blame him ... He didn't score the fight," he explained. "That's the worst I've ever been dealt in my life. They put the silver medal around my neck and I took it right off. I won't put it around my neck ever again." Jones was later named the 'best stylist' boxer at the Games, a remarkable feat given he failed to win gold.

THE AFTERMATH

The media was quick to take up Jones' cause, but to no avail. *The New York Times* declared, "Jones was robbed of his gold medal by corrupt and partisan judges. He outboxed, outfought and outshone the other man in the ring." Under intense media pressure, The International Olympic Committee launched an investigation, releasing its findings in 1997. It found that two of the judges who voted against Jones had been lavishly hosted by the South Koreans in the lead-up to the Olympics. All of the judges received bans and the two who were wined and dined by the Koreans were ousted for life. This led for calls for the decision against Jones to be reversed, but the IOC would not go that far. The outcry over the bout resulted in the IOC making changes to the way bouts are scored, however, using new technology.

After the investigation in 1997, the IOC presented Jones with its Olympic Order, giving him a silver bracelet in a ceremony that reduced Jones to tears. Roy Jones Jr went on to become one of the greatest professional fighters of all time, and the first man to win the world heavyweight crown after starting his career as a middleweight. He lives in hope that the IOC will one day reverse the decision and award him the gold medal. Park Si-Hun never entered the professional ranks and retired soon after the 1988 Olympics. In recent years, he has helped coach the South Korean national team.

A MATCH MADE IN HEAVEN, 2008

THE BACKGROUND

It seemed the perfect marriage – two sporting superstars finding love in their fifties, and settling down together after turbulent times in their personal lives over the years. Golf great Greg Norman and tennis legend Chris Evert seemed to have it all, and their love affair made headlines around the world when it became public, early in 2007.

Norman, Australia's most famous golfer and one of the wealthiest sportsmen in the world, had been linked with British tennis star Sue Barker in the 1970s, before marrying flight attendant Laura Andrassy in 1981. The pair settled in Florida, had two children and were married for over 25 years before Norman announced they would be seeking a divorce.

"Laura and I will be getting a divorce and both of us obviously want to have our privacy protected," Norman said in May 2006. "It's not the nicest of things to go through ... we are going to do this amicably. We both want to do it amicably. That's the best way of going about it. We've had 27 years together and, absolutely, we will remain friends." Andrassy is believed to have received over $100 million in the settlement.

When the relationship between Chris Evert, formerly Andrassy's friend, and Norman was revealed the following year, Andrassy spoke out on television. "I've never, ever encountered a woman like that before ... I don't have respect for her as a woman. She's a nonentity in my life," she said of Evert. Norman fired back via current affairs program *60 Minutes*: "To me it [Andrassay's TV interview] was a very deliberate attempt to make my life that much more miserable. As a matter of fact, she actually came out with a quote, she said, I'm going to make his life miserable 'for the rest of his life.'"

Evert's former husband, champion skier Andy Mill, also commented on the turn of events. "Greg Norman at one time was my best friend," he said. "I would have taken a bullet for this guy. But I didn't realise he was the one who was going to pull the trigger."

THE SCANDAL

Norman and Evert announced they were getting married and the pair tied the knot in a lavish ceremony in the Bahamas in June 2008. To the outside world, they seemed blissfully happy, with Evert serving as Norman's caddie when he came within a whisker of winning the 2008 British Open, in what would have been a fairytale, coming 22 years after he won the title for the first time.

But just 15 months after they married, Norman set the tabloid newspapers into another frenzy, when he announced he and Evert were set to divorce. In a prepared statement, Norman said they would "remain friends and supportive of one another's family".

But Evert was far from friendly in an interview with *Woman's Day* magazine soon afterwards. "I had no idea it was coming. No idea," Evert claimed. "It wasn't talked about, ever . . . Never in a million years did I imagine it would end up like this."

THE AFTERMATH

Evert swore off falling in love again after the split. Norman recovered far more quickly – in October 2010, less than a year after filing for divorce from Evert in a Florida court, Norman announced he was engaged to interior decorator Kirsten Kutner. The Australian-born Kutner had been friends with Norman for many years. The couple married a month later in the British Virgin Islands. His son, Gregory Jr, served as best man.

Andrassy weighed in on the high-profile divorce, giving the tabloids more fodder. "Well, it didn't come as a surprise," she said, when she learned Norman and Evert were separated. "So soon was the surprise. I think we all knew [that it would end in divorce] . . . We didn't have high hopes for it. But they had been telling everyone how much in love they were, so everybody thought it would last a little longer than this.

"I said to Andy [Mill] when I spoke to him today, 'It's like a bad movie – and we're in it!'"

VET'S HORSE SWITCH, 1977

THE BACKGROUND

Mark Gerard loved horses. Born in Brooklyn in New York in 1934, he studied to be a veterinarian at Cornell University and helped pay for his tuition by working as an exercise rider for horses at the Belmont Park track. When he began working as a vet after graduating, he quickly established himself as a leader in his field. Among his "clients" were three horses that won the Kentucky Derby – the legendary Secretariat, Ridge and Canoero II. Another horse in his care was Kelso, a thoroughbred rated the fourth-best American horse of the 20th century.

Gerard's love of horses took him to South America, where he established a lucrative side business, importing thoroughbreds to the USA. In 1977, he bought two colts from Uruguay with vastly different track records, but who looked strikingly similar to the untrained eye. The first was Cinzano, the Uruguay Horse of the Year in 1976, regarded as one of the finest colts the country had ever produced. The other, Lebon, was a plodder that had not won a race in nearly a year.

In September 1977, Lebon was entered in the final race at Belmont Park on a murky Friday afternoon and, at juicy odds of 57-1, romped home to score an easy win. Most punters were stunned by the win, but not Mark Gerard. He bet nearly $2,000 on Lebon to win and get a place, walking away from the track with $77,920 in cash, stuffed in a brown paper bag.

THE SCANDAL

There were whispers about a sting, with the bookies left licking their wounds from Gerard's plunge after Lebon won by a remarkable four lengths. The form showed Lebon had raced just once in the US before his triumph, finishing 11th in a field of 12 horses. But the suspicions came to nought until three weeks later, when a Uruguayan sports writer called Belmont Park officials after seeing a photo of Lebon in a newspaper. The reporter immediately recognised that the horse was, in fact, Cinzano, and not Lebon; although the horses were similar, they had different-shaped white stars on their faces. An angry woman had allegedly tipped off the journalist about the switch, having bet $10,000 on Lebon to win that first race and lost her money.

Cinzano (or Lebon) was seized by the authorities and placed under 24-hour guard until they could determine his real identity. Investigations revealed that Lebon had been put down after suffering a fractured skull soon after arriving in the United States. His carcass was sold to a fat renderer, and it was then the identities of the horses were switched. On top of his winnings, Gerard also collected a $150,000 insurance payout on Cinzano. Gerard's girlfriend reportedly flushed some of the winning tickets down the toilet, because she was concerned cashing them all would create unwanted attention. Gerard took the risk, however, and was recognised by a runner, who was sent to the money room to collect his winnings.

After the scandal was uncovered, Gerard was charged with making a false entry in a "contest of speed", a misdemeanour. He had his license suspended by the New York State Racing and Wagering Board and spent eight months in jail in New York State's Nassau County. He was acquitted of defrauding the insurance company Lloyd's of London.

THE AFTERMATH

After his prison sentence was completed, Gerard's days as a vet to the rich and famous of the racing industry were over. He maintained his association with horses, however, training polo ponies in both Florida and California. It was while he was at work in June 2011 that Gerard suffered a stroke. He died in hospital in Miami several days later, aged 76.

Cinzano was barred from ever racing at the elite level again. Racing fans couldn't help noticing the irony – the mastermind behind the scheme got less than a year, while the horse was ousted for life. Cinzano was purchased by a Randolph Rouse of Arlington County, a fox hunter who was hoping to use him as a steeplechaser. But officials put a stop to that, so Rouse rode the colt in point-to-point races in Virginia. The races were not for money. In 10 events over two years, Rouse and Cinzano were never beaten. Cinzano died in 1999, aged 26 ... a champion.

VICK'S BAD DOG DAYS, 2007

THE BACKGROUND

US footballer Michael Vick grew up in tough circumstances. When he was born in 1980, his parents were unmarried teenagers and he spent his early years in a public housing project in Virginia. Crime was common in the area, with drug deals and drive-by shootings a part of everyday life.

Vick learned early on that if he was going to make something of his life, it would be through his athletic ability. "Sports kept me off the streets," he said in an interview looking back on his childhood. "It kept me from getting into what was going on, the bad stuff. Lots of guys I knew had bad problems."

A fine all-round athlete, Vick quickly became a football rising star. He excelled at Homer L. Ferguson High School in his hometown of Newport News. The school shut down when he was 16, but he proved just as good at Warwick High School. Colleges fell over themselves to sign the classy quarterback, with Vick deciding on Virginia Tech. He excelled in his first year, finishing third in the Heisman Trophy, equalling the highest-ever place by a freshman to that point.

Vick left after his sophomore year to join the pros, becoming the first African-American quarterback to be chosen first overall in the NFL draft when he signed a huge contract with Atlanta. Vick's brilliant running game quickly made him a favourite with Falcons fans and he dominated many games with his speed and skill.

THE SCANDAL

In April of 2007, just when he was at the peak of his powers and among the best-known players in the NFL, Vick was implicated in an illegal dog fighting racket. The ring operated out of a property owned by Vick in Surry County, Virginia, ironically called Bad Newz Kennels. After initially denying all charges, Vick changed his tune four months later. When three of his associates were prepared to testify that Vick played a key role in the dog fighting syndicate, and even executed under-performing animals personally, Vick declared he would "accept full responsibility" for his role and pleaded guilty to federal conspiracy charges.

The NFL acted swiftly, suspending Vick indefinitely without pay for breaking its player code of conduct. NFL commissioner Roger Goodall hit Vick with the harsh punishment, unusual for a first-time offender, because he had funded the gambling side of the ring and behaved in a manner that was "not only illegal, but also cruel and reprehensible". Vick was also charged with testing positive to marijuana, which was in violation of his pretrial release terms.

Eventually, in November 2007, Vick was jailed for 23 months by US District Court judge Henry Hudson. The judge added five months to the term he would usually have imposed, because Vick continually lied about his involvement in the ring before cracking under intense grilling by the FBI. He served the majority of his incarceration in the Leavenworth prison in Kansas. Vick, said to be the highest paid player in the NFL and the face of the Falcons franchise when the scandal began, lost millions of dollars in endorsements.

THE AFTERMATH

The Falcons demanded that Vick reimburse them for a sum close to $20 million out of a massive $37 million bonus the franchise had paid him. The case went to arbitration, with Vick ending up having to pay the club around $19.97 million. The hefty penalty was imposed because the arbitrator ruled that Vick knew he was involved in an illegal activity when he signed a new deal with the Falcons in 2004, with a portion of his bonus money actually funding the dog fighting operation.

By July 2008, Vick filed for bankruptcy. In June 2009, the Falcons released Vick, making the fallen star an unrestricted free agent. After serving his time in prison, Vick considered playing in Canada, but was thrown a lifeline by the Philadelphia Eagles, who signed him to a one-year deal in August 2009. He was activated the following month and in December, after a series of strong displays, won the Ed Block Courage Award, a prize voted on by his Eagles team-mates. The award is given to players who show "the principles of sportsmanship and courage". By the following season, he was the Eagles' regular quarterback, replacing Donovan McNabb, who was traded to Washington. In November 2010, he became the first player to pass for three touchdowns and rush for two touchdowns in the first half of an NFL game, and holds a host of other NFL records. He works as an unlikely animal rights activist, saying he hopes others learn from his mistakes.

Bibliography

'Black Sox' life ban, 1919
1. 2003, 'The Chicago Black Sox banned from baseball', ESPN, November 19, viewed 2013.
2. Gandil, A 1956, 'This is My Story of the Black Sox Series', *Sports Illustrated*, September 17, viewed 2013.
3. Linder, D 2010, *The Black Sox Trial: An Account (1979)*, University of Missouri Kansas City School of Law, viewed 2013, <http://law2.umkc.edu/faculty/projects/ftrials/blacksox/blacksoxaccount.html>.

Pakistan cricketers jailed, 2011
1. Marks, V 2010, 'Pakistan embroiled in no-ball betting scandal against England', *The Guardian,* 29 August, viewed 2013.
2. 2010, 'Two Pakistan players issued notices before scandal', *Cricinfo (ESPN)*, 7 September viewed 2013.
3. 2010, 'Salman Butt appeals against ICC suspension', *Cricinfo (ESPN)*, 29 September, viewed 2013.
4. 2011, 'Pakistan trio banned by cricket's anti-corruption body', *CNN,* 5 February, viewed 2013.
5. 2011, 'Pakistan cricketers guilty of betting scam', *BBC News*, 1 November, viewed 2013.

Fine Cotton's painted substitute, 1984
1. White, S 2010, 'Haiden Haytana still paying for the Fine Cotton betting scandal', *The Adelaide Advertiser,* August 13, viewed 2013.
2. 2009, 'Fine Cotton, horse in racing scandal, dies', *Courier Mail*, February 19, viewed 2013.

Bodyline, 1932
1. Cashman, R, Franks, W, Maxwell, J, Sainsbury, E, Stoddart, B, Weaver, A; Webster, R, 1997, *The A–Z of Australian Cricketers*, Oxford University Press, Melbourne.
2. Frith, D 2002, *Bodyline Autopsy*, ABC Books, Sydney.
3. Pollard, J 1988, *The Bradman Years: Australian Cricket 1918–48*, Harpercollins, North Ryde.

NFL star's dead girlfriend hoax, 2013
1. 2013, 'Hoaxer was in love with Manti Te'o', *ESPN,* 31 January, viewed 2013.
2. 2013, 'Photo woman: Tuiasosopo confessed', *ESPN,* 25 January, viewed 2013.
3. 2013, 'Notre Dame Statement: Manti 'Te'o Was Victim of A Hoax', CBS, January 16, viewed 2013.

NBA ref's betting shame, 2007
1. 2007, 'Donaghy under investigation for betting on NBA games', *ESPN*, July 20, viewed 2013.
2. 2008, 'Donaghy sentenced to 15 months in prison in gambling scandal', *ESPN*, July 29, viewed 2013.
3. 2007, 'FBI probes whether NBA ref bet on games', *USA Today*, July 20, viewed 2013.
4. 2007, 'NBA ref scandal is 'wakeup call,' Stern says', *USA Today*, August 16, viewed 2013.

O.J. escapes murder conviction, 1995
1. 1996, 'List of the evidence in the O.J. Simpson murder trial', *USA Today,* October 18, viewed 2013, <http://usatoday30.usatoday.com/news/index/nns25.htm>.
2. 1997, 'Jury unanimous: Simpson is liable', *CNN,* February 4, viewed 2013.
3. Gleick, E 1996, 'O.J. Simpson feels the heat', *Time*, December 2, viewed 2013.
4. McClam, E 2006, 'Publisher Calls Book O.J.'s "Confession", *Fox News*, November 15, viewed 2013.

The Nazi Olympics, 1936
1. *The Facade of Hospitality*, The Nazi Olympics Berlin 1936 Exhibition, United States Holocaust Memorial Museum, viewed 2013, <www.ushmm.org/museum/exhibit/online/olympics/>.
2. Mandell, RD 1987, *The Nazi Olympics*, University of Illinois Press.
3. Walter, G 1998, *Berlin Games: How Hitler Stole the Olympic Dream*, John Murray, London.

Death at sea, 1998
1. 1998, 'Launceston men die in Sydney-Hobart', *The Examiner,* 28 December, viewed 2013.
2. 2004, 'Race storm ends for maligned skipper', *Sydney Morning Herald*, 3 April, viewed 2013.
3. 2005, 'Families vindicated as yacht club settles race case', *Sydney Morning Herald*, 12 October, viewed 2013.

Accusation of on-pitch insult, 2011
1. 2002, 'Terry faces England exile', *BBC Sport*, 18 January, viewed 2013.
2. 2012, 'Regina v John Terry: Judgment', Judiciary of England Wales, *BBC News*, 13 July, viewed 2013, http://news.*BBC*.co.uk/2/shared/bsp/hi/pdfs/13_07_12_r_v_john_terry.pdf.
3. 2012, 'John Terry banned and fined by FA over Anton Ferdinand incident', *BBC Sport*, 27 September, viewed 2013.
4. 2012, 'John Terry stripped of England captaincy by FA ahead of racism trial', *The Guardian*, 3 February, viewed 2013.

Tiger's fall from grace, 2009
1. Dahlberg, T 2009, 'Two weeks that shattered the legend of Tiger Woods', *Associated Press,* December 12, viewed 2013.
2. 2009, 'Tiger Woods admits 'transgressions', apologises', *Reuters*, December 2, viewed 2013.
3. Woods, T 2009, 'Statement from Tiger Woods', *TigerWoods.com*, November 29, <http://web.tigerwoods.com/news/article/200911297726222/news/>.

Tragedy at Hillsborough, 1989

1. 2009, 'Hillsborough: the disaster that changed football', *The Times*, 13 April, viewed 2013.
2. 2009, 'How the Hillsborough disaster happened', *BBC News*, 14 April, viewed 2013.
3. 2009, 'Hillsborough timeline', *The Daily Telegraph*, 14 April, viewed 2013.
4. 2009, 'It was a tragic waste of life', *The Sun*, 14 April, viewed 2013.

Ben Johnson drugs scandal, 1988

1. Harvey, R 1987, 'Lewis Claims Some Medalists Using Illegal Drugs', *Los Angeles Times*, September 6, viewed 2013.
2. 1986, 'Johnson, Bubka Set Indoor Records', *Washington Post*, January 16, viewed 2013.
3. Slot, O 2003, 'Ambition, naivety and tantalising prospect of inheriting the world', *The Times*, September 22, viewed 2013.

Figure skating vote trade, 2002

1. Dampf, A 2002, 'Taivanchik Hearing Ordered to Stay Put', *The St Petersburg Times*, 13 August, viewed 2013.
2. Salt Lake Organizing Committee 2002, 'Official Report of the XIX Olympic Winter Games', viewed 2013, <http://www.la84foundation.org/6oic/OfficialReports/2002/2002v1.pdf>.

'Dis-Onischenko', the KGB Olympic Cheat, 1976

1. Henderson, J 2001, 'The 10 Greatest Cheats in Sporting History', *The Guardian,* 8 July, viewed 2013.
2. Walker, T 2012, 'Olympic controversies', *ESPN UK,* August 3, viewed 2013.

Greek stars kicked out of Games, 2004

1. 2009, 'Trial for Greek sprinters postponed', *USA TODAY*, February 5, viewed 2013.
2. 2006, 'Sprint duo drop drugs ban appeals', *BBC Sport*, 26 June, viewed 2013.

College basketball point shaving, 1951

1. Goldstein, J 2003, 'Explosion: 1951 scandals threaten college hoops', *ESPN Classics*, November 19, viewed 2013.
2. 1951, 'The Big Money', *Time*, February 26, viewed 2013.
3. *City Dump: The Story of the 1951 CCNY Basketball Scandal* 1998, motion picture, Time Warner.

'Dolly' tackles Apartheid, 1968

1. Williamson, M 2008, 'The D'Oliveira Affair', *ESPN Cricinfo*, 13 September, viewed 2013.
2. Bruce, K 2002, 'The Sports Boycott and Cricket: The Cancellation of the 1970 South African Tour of England', South African Historical Journal, vol. 46, issue 1, viewed 2013.

Warne's diet pill ban, 2003

1. 2006, 'The finest leg-spinner the world has ever seen', *ESPN Cricinfo Australia*, 20 December, viewed 2013.
2. 2003, 'Drug test halts Warne's World Cup', *The Age*, 12 February, viewed 2013.
3. 2003, 'Warne's mum key element in probe', *ESPN Cricinfo*, 20 February, viewed 2013.
4. 2003, 'ACB Anti-Doping Committee suspends Shane Warne', *ESPN Cricinfo*, February 22, viewed 2013.

Marion Jones drug disgrace, 2007

1. Williams, L 2006, 'Sprinter Jones failed drug test', *San Francisco Chronicle*, August 19, viewed 2013.
2. Zinser, L and Schmidt, MS 2007, 'Jones Admits to Doping and Enters Guilty Plea', *New York Times*, October 6, viewed 2013.
3. 2008, 'Disgraced sprinter Jones reports to jail', *AFP*, March 7, viewed 2013.
4. Shipley, A 2010 'Marion Jones returns to sport with the WNBA's Tulsa Shock', *The Washington Post*, 16 May, viewed 2013.

Hansie Cronje's cricket fixing, 2000

1. UCBSA 2000, 'United Cricket Board of South Africa statement on match fixing allegations', *ESPN Cricinfo*, 8 April, viewed 2013.
2. Robinson, P 2000, 'Cronje finally comes clean', *ESPN Cricinfo*, 15 June, viewed 2013.
3. 2006, 'Cronje inquest opens', *Sydney Morning Herald*, 8 August, viewed 2013.

East German unwitting doper's sex change, 1997

1. Harding, L 2005, 'Forgotten victims of East German doping take their battle to court', *The Guardian*, November 1, viewed 2013.
2. Longman, Jere 2004, 'East German Steroids' Toll: 'They Killed Heidi'', *The New York Times*. 26 January, viewed 2013.

Footballer's Thai prison hell, 1978

1. *Rugby League Week* magazine, July–August 1982.

Olympic runner hitches a ride, 1904

1. Miller, M 2004, 'Olympics flashback: 1904 marathon a joke of a race', *Madison.com*, 25 August, viewed 2013.

Skategate assault, 1994

1. Swift, EM 1994, 'Anatomy of a Plot', *Sports Illustrated*, February 14, viewed 2013.
2. 1994, 'Kerrigan Attacker and Accomplice Sent to Jail', *The New York Times*, May 17, viewed 2013.
3. Couch, G 2000, 'Harding's new image takes a beating', *Chicago Sun-Times*, February 27, viewed 2013.

Tyson goes feral, 1997

1. 1997, 'Tyson Disqualified for biting Holyfield's Ears', *New York Times*, 29 June, viewed 2013.
2. 1997, 'Tyson banned for life', *AP (via Slam Boxing)*, July 9, viewed 2013.
3. 'Tyson jailed over road rage', *BBC News*, February 6, 1999
4. 1999, 'Tyson files for bankruptcy', *BBC Sport*, August 3, viewed 2013.

Ayrton Senna's tragic death, 1994

1. Thomson, I 1994, 'Suddenly, Death Returns to Formula One Auto Racing'. *The New York Times*, 2 May, viewed 2013.
2. 1994, 'Formula One circuit faces tough questions', *The Milwaukee Journal*, 3 May.
3. 1994, 'Grand Prix's poor safety record criticized after pair of fatalities', *Allegheny Times*, 2 May, viewed 2013.
4. 1995, 'Report on Senna's death ready', *New Straits Times*, 25 February, viewed 2013.

Women's golf ball-moving accusation, 1972

1. 1972, 'Blalock files LPGA lawsuit', *Park City News*, June 1.
2. 1972, 'Court order for Blalock', *The Phoenix*, June 3.

Diver's HIV revelation, 1994

1. 2010, 'Greg Louganis Interview', *Ability Magazine*, viewed 2013.
2. 2009, 'Life for Louganis more about dogs than diving', *The San Diego Union Tribune*, June 13, viewed 2013.

The underarm bowling saga, 1981

1. Knight, B 2004, 'Underarm incident was a cry for help: Greg Chappell', *ABC Local Radio* (transcript), 31 January, viewed 2013.
2. Swanton, W 2006, '25 years along, Kiwi bat sees funnier side of it', *The Age*, 23 January, viewed 2013.

Media mogul hijacks Australian cricket, 1977

1. Haigh, G 1993, *The Cricket War – The Inside Story of Kerry Packer's World Series Cricket*, Text Publishing, Melbourne.
2. McFarline, P 1977, *A Game Divided,* Hutchinson, Sydney.

Italian soccer 'betting-gate', 2011

1. 2011, 'Giuseppe Signori held in football fixing probe', *BBC Sport*, 1 June, viewed 2013.
2. 2012, 'Conte also under investigation, Mauri and Milanetto arrested', *La Gazzetta dello Sport,* 28 May, viewed 2013.
3. 2012, 'Premier: Suspend soccer in Italy', *ESPN*, 29 May.
4. 2012, 'Euro 2012: Cesare Prandelli has no problem if Italy withdraw', *BBC*, June 2, viewed 2013.

McLaren employees spy on Ferrari, 2007

1. Cooper, A 2007, 'Analysis: the remarkable Stepneygate saga', Autosport.com, 10 July, viewed 2013.
2. Noble, J 2007, 'Stepney moves in Ferrari reshuffle', *Autosport.com,* 23 February, viewed 2013.
3. Goren, B and Noble, J 2007, 'Spy case court hearing adjourned', *Autosport.com*, 10 July, viewed 2013.
4. Gorman, E 2007, 'Coughlan accused of 'disgraceful' behaviour', *The Times,* 10 July, viewed 2013.
5. 2007, 'McLaren hit with constructors' ban', *BBC News*, 13 September, viewed 2013.

Yugoslav basketball's civil war, 1990

1. *Once Brothers,* 2010, TV documentary, 30 for 30 series, ESPN.
2. Rodrick, S 2005, 'Spirit of the Game', *ESPN The Magazine,* August 8, viewed 2013.

Budd and Decker collide, 1984

1. Wooldridge, I 2003, 'Zola deserves warm welcome after all we put her through', *Daily Mail*, April 9, viewed 2013.
2. Budd, Z and Eley, H 1989, *Zola: The Autobiography of Zola Budd*, Partridge Press.

German soccer ref thrown into jail, 2005

1. Macintyre, D 2005, 'Ref who stole football's soul', *Sunday World*, March 7, viewed 2013.
2. 2006, 'Prosecutor urges overturning Hoyzer conviction', *Reuters*, 29 November, viewed 2013.

Jim Thorpe stripped of his medals, 1913

1. Smithsonian Institute, 'Jim Thorpe: All-Around Athlete and American Indian Advocate', viewed 2013, <http://amhistory.si.edu/sports/exhibit/champions/thorpe/index.cfm>.
2. 1953, 'Jim Thorpe Is Dead On West Coast at 64', *The New York Times*, March 29, viewed 2013.
3. 2004, 'Jim Thorpe cruelly treated by authorities', *Sports Illustrated*, August 8, viewed 2013.
4. Updyke, R K 1997, *Jim Thorpe, the Legend Remembered*, Pelican, Gretna, LA.

Phantom horse wins in fog, 1990

1. 1990, 'Rider Sylvester Carmouche Galloped Out of the Bayou Mists', *People Magazine*, May 14, viewed 2013.
2. 1991, 'Jockey convicted of Hiding in the Fog', *Associated Press*, May 14, viewed 2013.
3. 1990, 'Jockey Faces Felony Charge', *Associated Press*, January 19, viewed 2013.

Ali refuses to be drafted, 1966

1. 1978, 'The Greatest' Is Gone', *TIME*, February 27, viewed 2013.
2. Reemstsma, J 1999, *More Than a Champion: The Style of Muhammad Ali*, Vintage, New York.
3. US Supreme Court Center 1971, 'Clay v. United States – 403 U.S. 698', viewed 2013, < https://supreme.justia.com/cases/federal/us/403/698/case.html>.
4. Hill, B 2005, 'Ali stirs conflicting emotions in hometown', *The Courier-Journal*, November 19, viewed 2013.

Paralympic frauds, 2000

1. 2000, 'Spain ordered to return golds', *BBC Sport*, 14 December, viewed 2013.
2. Reilly, R 2000, 'Paralympic Paradox', *Sports Illustrated*, 11 December, viewed 2013.
3. 2009, 'Intellectual disability ban ends', *BBC News*, 21 November, viewed 2013.

Armstrong confesses web of lies, 2013

1. Weislo, L 2013, 'Index of Lance Armstrong doping allegations over the years', *Cycling News*, January 16, viewed 2013, <http://www.cyclingnews.com/features/index-of-lance-armstrong-doping-allegations-over-the-years>.
2. 2005, 'Armstrong on newspaper's accusations: "This thing

stinks'", *CNN*, 26 August, viewed 2013.
3. Seaton, M 2012, 'Lance Armstrong and USADA's doping charges', *The Guardian*, 14 June, viewed 2013.

Harlequins cheat with fake blood, 2009
1. 2009, 'Quins escape further action in bloodgate scandal', *AFP*, 24 August, viewed 2013.
2. Roycroft-Davis, C 2009, 'Harlequins have let down all of rugby', *The Times*, 18 August, viewed 2013.
3. Souster, M 2009, 'Dean Richards handed worldwide ban', *The Times*, 18 August, viewed 2013.

Black power salute, 1968
1. Eastley, T 2012, 'John Carlos: No Australian finer than Peter Norman', *Australian Broadcasting Corporation*, 21 August, viewed 2013.
2. Lewis, R 2006, 'Caught in Time: Black Power salute, Mexico, 1968', *The Sunday Times*, 8 October, viewed 2013.
3. Wise, M 2006, 'Clenched fists, helping hand', *The Washington Post*, October 5, viewed 2013.

Soccer star murdered after own goal, 1999
1. *The Two Escobars* 2009, television documentary, 30 for 30 series, ESPN TV.
2. Davison, P 1994, 'Medellin mourns its murdered sports star', *The Independent*, July 4.
3. Almond, E 1994, 'World Cup USA '94: Unforgivable', *Los Angeles Times*, July 3, viewed 2013.
4. Chua-Eoan, H 1994, 'The Case of the Fatal Goal', *Time Magazine*, July 11, viewed 2013.
5. Small, G 2008, 'Remembering the Black Power protest', *The Guardian*, 9 July, viewed 2013.
6. 2005, 'Columbian Goalie's Killer Released Early', *MSNBC Sports*, 6 October, viewed 2013.

NFL Saints' bounty blues, 2010
1. Maske, M 2012, 'NFL to investigate Redskins over bounty allegations under Gregg Williams', *The Washington Post*, 4 March, viewed 2013.
2. Silver, M 2012, 'Gregg Williams instructed Saints during speech to injure Niners offensive players', *Yahoo Sports*, 5 April, viewed 2013.
3. 2012, 'Bills had bounty system under Gregg Williams, players say', *The Buffalo News*, 3 March, viewed 2013.

Miracle in the Andes, 1972
1. Parrado, N and Rause, V 2006, *Miracle in the Andes: 72 Days on the Mountain and My Long Trek Home*, Crown Publishers, USA.
2. Read, PP 1974, *Alive: The Story of the Andes Survivors*, J. B. Lippincott Company, USA.
3. Viven 2013, *The Andes Incident*, www.viven.com.uy, viewed 2013.

Protesting vandals ruin cricket Test, 1975
1. Mallett, A and Chappell, I 2005, *Chapelli Speaks Out*, Allen and Unwin, Australia.
2. Collis, I 2012, *Cricket Through the Decades*, New Holland Publishers, Sydney.
3. 1975, 'Davis campaigners stop Test match', *BBC*, 19 August, viewed 2013.

Nazi gender bender exposure, 1938
1. 2009, 'The Jewish jumper and the male imposter', *BBC News*, 9 September, viewed 2013.
2. 2010, 'How Dora the Man competed in the woman's high jump', *Der Spiegel*, 31 August, viewed 2013.
3. 'Dora Ratjen', www.sports-reference.com, viewed 2013, <http://www.sports-reference.com/olympics/athletes/ra/dora-ratjen-1.html>.

Jordan defects to baseball, 1994
1. 'Michael Jordan', NBA Encyclopedia, viewed 2013, <www.nba.com/history/players/jordan_bio.html>.
2. Porter, DL 2007, *Michael Jordan: A Biography*, Greenwood Press, USA.

War in Hungary, war in the water, 1956
1. 'Melbourne 1956', www.Olympic.org, viewed 2013, <www.olympic.org/photos/melbourne-1956>.
2. Fimrite, R 2007, 'A bloody war that spilled into the pool', *Sports Illustrated*, 24 March, viewed 2013.
3. 1956, 'Cold War violence erupts at Melbourne Olympics', *Sydney Morning Herald*, 7 December.

Cricket coach's suspicious death, 2007
1. Meher-Homji, K 2012, *Cricket Conflicts and Controversies*, New Holland Publishers, Sydney. 2. 2007, 'Coach Woolmer "was not murdered"', *BBC News*, 2 June, viewed 2013.
3. 2007, 'Obituary: Bob Woolmer', *The Times*, 19 March, viewed 2013.

Jimmy Gauld soccer fix confession, 1964
1. Brown, N, 'Jimmy Gauld', Post-War English & Scottish Football League A – Z Player's Database, viewed 2013, <www.neilbrown.newcastlefans.com/player/jimmygauld.htm>.
2. Jackson, J 2004, 'Triumph and Despair', *The Observer*, 4 July, viewed 2013.
3. Broadbent, R 2006, 'Swan still reduced to tears by the fix that came unstuck', *The Times*, 22 July, viewed 2013.

'Busby's Babes' air disaster, 1958
1. Reeves, J 2012, *The Battle for Manchester*, New Holland Publishers, Sydney.
2. 'Busby babes: 1950s', About Man Utd, viewed 2013, <www.aboutmanutd.com/man-u-history/busby-babes.html>.

Colts skip town, 1984
1. Gibbons, M 2006, 'Baltimore Colts: A Team for Ages', *Press Box*, 7 September, viewed 2013.
2. 'Baltimore Colts' (1953–84), *Sports E-Cyclopedia*, viewed 2013,

<http://www.sportsecyclopedia.com/nfl/balticolts/baltcolts.html>

Seles' on-court stabbing, 1993

1. Adams, WL 2011, '30 legends of women's tennis: past, present and future – Monica Seles', *Time*, 22 June, viewed 2013.
2. Jenkins, S 1993, 'Monica Seles attack', *Sports Illustrated*, 10 May, viewed 2013.
3. Seles, M and Richardson, NA 1996, *Moncia Seles: From Fear to Victory*, Harpercollins, USA.

The Shergar kidnap mystery, 1983

1. Bedford, J 2013, 'Shergar: The day the wonder horse was stolen', *BBC News*, 8 February, viewed 2013.
2. 2004, 'New light on Shergar mystery', *The Age*, 14 March.
3. Alderson, A 2008, 'The truth about Shergar racehorse kidnapping', *The Telegraph*, 27 January, viewed 2013.

Grobbelaar's 'Mr Fixit' charges, 1994

1. Gysin, C 2002, 'Grobbelaar's hollow victory earns him just £1 in damages', *Daily Mail*, 25 October.
2. Jackson, J 2005, 'Triumph and Despair: Bruce Grobbelaar', *The Observer,* 5 June, viewed 2013.
3. 'Judgments – Grobbelaar (Appellant) v News Group Newspapers Ltd and Another (Respondents)', Parliament UK, viewed 2013, <http://www.publications.parliament.uk/pa/ld200102/ldjudgmt/jd021024/grobb-1.htm>

Massacre at Munich, 1972

1. Calahan, A 1995, 'Countering Terrorism: The Israeli Response to the 1972 Munich Olympic Massacre and the development of Independent Covert Action Teams', thesis, viewed 2013, <https://www.fas.org/irp/eprint/calahan.htm>.
2. Jonas, G 2005, 'Vengeance: The True Story of Israeli Counter-Terrorist Team', Simon and Schuster, USA.
3. 2012, 'The Munich Massacre Remembered' video, *BBC News*, 4 September, viewed 2013.

Suffragette's fatal sacrifice, 1913

1. 'Emily Davison (1872–1913), *BBC History*, viewed 2013, <www.bbc.co.uk/history/historic_figures/davison_emily.shtml>.
2. 1913, 'Emily Davison's death', *Morning Post*, 5 June.

Italian marathon hero disqualified, 1903

1. 1905, 'A New Marathon Champion: Frederick Lorz of the Mohawk Athletic Club of New York Captured the Great Run in an Exciting Contest', *Boston Evening Transcript*, April 20, viewed 2013.
2. Hanc, J 2004, 'The Worst of the Modern Olympics Was Held ... ?' *Newsday*, 25 August, viewed 2013.
3. Wallechinsky, D 1984, *The Complete Book of the Olympics*, Viking Press.

Black Sunday, 1920

1. Leeson, D 2003, 'Death in the Afternoon: The Croke Park Massacre', *Canadian Journal of History,* vol. 38, no. 1.

Olympic pin-up girl turns escort, 2012

1. 2012, 'US Olympian's Secret Life as Las Vegas Escort', *The Smoking Gun*, December 20, viewed 2013.
2. Woulfe, N 2012, 'Suzy Favor Hamilton, Olympian Turned Hooker, Could Be Caught up in FBI Probe', *Radar Online*, December 22, viewed 2013.

University football team's 'death penalty', 1986

1. White, GS 1989, 'Gridiron Greed', *The New York Times*, October 22, viewed 2013.
2. Whitford, D 1989, *A Payroll to Meet: A Story of Greed, Corruption, and Football at SMU*, Macmillan, USA.

Woman dies after drugs with hero, 2000

1. 2005, 'Ablett's Hall of Fame exile to end', *ABC Sport*, 2 June, viewed 2013.
2. 2003, 'Revealed: What took place in the hotel room', *The Age*, March 1, viewed 2013.

Giants steal signs via telescope, 1951

1. Boswell, T 2001, 'Giants stole the pennant! Giants stole the pennant!' *Los Angeles TImes,* February 4, viewed 2013.
2. Anderson, D 2001, 'Branca Knew '51 Giants Stole Signs', *The New York Times*, February 1, viewed 2013.

'Chucker' pressured out of cricket, 1963

1. Benaud, R 1998, *Anything But . . . An Autobiography*, Hodder and Staunton, Australia.
2. Haigh, G 1997, *The Summer Game: Australian Test Cricket 1949–1971*, Melbourne.

Gold medal winner's gender secret, 1980

1. 1981, 'Report Says Stella Walsh had Male Sex Organs', The New York Times, 22 January, viewed 2013.
2. 'Walasiewicz, Stanislawa' 2006, *Encyclopaedia Britannica.*

Pete Rose banned, 1989

1. Chass, M 1988, 'Pete Rose Is Suspended 30 Days', *The New York Times*, May 3, viewed 2013.
2. 2002, 'Dowd: Rose "probably" bet against Reds while manager', *ESPN News*, June 16, viewed 2013.

NFL's video spies exposed, 2006

1. 2007, 'Belichick draws $500,000 fine, but avoids suspension', *ESPN*, 14 July, viewed 2013.
2. English, B 2007 'After bruising year, Belichick opens up', *Boston Globe*, 4 March, viewed 2013.

The Rosie Ruiz shortcut, 1979

1. Moore, K 1980, 'Mastery and Mystery', *Sports Illustrated*, 28 April, viewed 2013.
2. 'Rosie Ruiz tries it steal the Boston Marathon', Running Times, 1 July 1980

Asthma drug confusion deals cruel blow, 1972
1. Amdur, N 1972, 'Of Gold and Drugs', *The New York Times*, September 4, viewed 2013.
2. 2001, 'Better late than never: Demont has gold medal acknowledged 29 years later', *Sports Illustrated*, January 30, viewed 2013.
3. Patrick, D 2001, 'De Mont redeemed after 29 years', *ESPN*, 6 December, viewed 2013.

Agassi comes clean, 2009
1. Agassi, A 2010, *Open: An Autobiography*, Vintage, London.
2. Molinaro, J 2010, 'Andre Agassi: Tennis' love affair with Agassi comes to an end', *CBC Sports*, 15 May, viewed 2013, <www.cbc.ca/sports/columns/newsmakers/andre-agassi.html>.

Australian football star poisoned, 1953
1. Sanders, N 1995, *The Thallium Enthusiasms and Other Australian Outrages*, Local Consumption Publications, Newtown.
2. Whiticker, A 2007, 'Another 12 Crimes That Shocked Australia', New Holland Publishers, Sydney.
3. 2005, 'Murder tried and true', *Sydney Morning Herald*, 2 October, viewed 2013.

Little League over-age scandal, 2001
1. 2001, 'He's 14: Almonte's team forfeits LLWS victories', *Sports Illustrated*, August 31, viewed 2013.
2. Thomsen, I and Llosa, LF 2001, 'One for the Ages', *Sports Illustrated*, 27 August, viewed 2013.

Piquet's alleged crash orders, 2008
1. Young, B 2009, 'Nelson Piquet can expect a paddock backlash for deliberately crashing his Renault at last year's Singapore Grand Prix', 22 September, viewed 2013.
2. Gorman, E 2010, 'FIA considers appeal after bans on Flavio Briatore has life ban lifted', *The Times*, 6 January, viewed 2013.

Tennis tanking fears, 2007
1. 2007, 'Tennis officials investigate irregular betting on match', *ESPN*, 3 August, viewed 2013.
2. 2007, 'Davydenko faces betting inquiry', *BBC Sport*, 27 August, viewed 2013.
3. 2008, 'Davydenko cleared of match-fixing', *BBC Sport*, 12 September, viewed 2013.

Baseball's dirty secret exposed, 2005
1. 2005, 'Canseco: Steroids made baseball career possible', *USA Today*, 13 February, viewed 2013.
2. Mitchell, G 2007, *Report to the Commissioner of Baseball of an Independent Investigation into the Illegal Use of Steroids and Other Performance Enhancing Substances by Players in Major League Baseball*, 13 December, viewed 2013, < http://files.mlb.com/mitchrpt.pdf>
3. 2009, 'A-Rod admits, regrets use of PEDs', *ESPN*, 10 February, viewed 2013.

Sailor's tragic hoax, 1968
1. Tomalin, N and Hall, R 2003, *The Strange Last Voyage of Donald Crowhurst*, Hodder & Stoughton, USA.
2. Harris, J 1981, *Without a Trace*, Atheneum, USA.

Assault in the ring, 1983
1. *Assault in the Ring* 2008, television documentary, HBO.
2. Mladnich, R 2008, 'Resto Comes Clean: He Knew Gloves Were Loaded', *The Sweet Science*, 6 April, viewed 2013.

War on the pitch, 1969
1. Kapuscinski, R and Brand, W (trans.) 1990, *The Soccer War*, Granta Books, London.
2. 2000, 'Soccer War, 1969', Wars of the World, December 16, viewed 2013, <www.onwar.com/aced/data/sierra/soccer1969.htm>.

Women 'invade' Lord's, 1998
1. 1999, 'MCC delivers first ten maidens', *BBC News*, March 16, viewed 2013.
2. Dugan, E 2008, 'Women cricketers fail to break through old boys' defensive block', *The Independent*, 28 September, viewed 2013.

Roy Jones Jr robbed, 1988
1. Mamet, D 1988, 'In Losing, a Boxer Won', *The New York Times*, 7 October.
2. Vecsey, G 1997, 'Sports of the Times; Nice Gesture Substitutes for Justice', *The New York Times*, 26 September, viewed 2013.

A match made in heaven, 2008
1. Byrne, F 2010, 'Chris Evert tells of shock at split from Greg Norman', *Herald Sun*, 5 July, viewed 2013.
2. Hellard, P 2007, 'Greg Norman betrayed best mate', *The Sunday Telegraph*, 19 August, viewed 2013.
3. Murray, J 2009, 'So what drove a wedge between Chris and Greg?', *Sunday Express*, 4 October, viewed 2013.
4. Howard, D 2009, 'Greg Norman and Chris Evert are narcissists says ex wife Laura Andrassy', *The Sunday Telegraph*, 4 October, viewed 2013.

Vet's horse switch, 1977
1. Shapiro, TR 2011, 'Mark Gerard, veterinarian at center of horse-swapping scheme, dies at 76', *The Washington Post*, 28 June, viewed 2013.
2. Christine, B 2011, 'Obituary: Mark Gerard dies at 76; prominent racetrack veterinarian', *Los Angeles Times*, 25 June, viewed 2013.

Vick's bad dog days, 2007
1. 2007, 'Vick to be sentenced Dec. 10 after guilty plea', *ESPN*, 28 August, viewed 2013.
2. 2007, 'Vick Indicted on Va. Dogfighting Charges', *Time.com*, 14 October, viewed 2013.

UK £12.99
US $16.99